Container Gardens

EASY GARDENS

Container Gardens

Daria Price Bowman

MetroBooks

MetroBooks

An Imprint of the Michael Friedman Publishing Group, Inc.

©2002 by Michael Friedman Publishing Group, Inc.

Library of Congress Cataloging-in-Publication Data

Bowman, Daria Price.
    Container gardens / Daria Price Bowman.
      p.cm.—(Easy gardens)
    Includes bibliographical references (p.) and index.
    ISBN 1-58663-086-5 (alk. paper)
      1. Container gardening. I. Title. II. Series.

SB418 .B69 2002
635.9'86—dc21

                                        20010440252

Editor: Susan Lauzau
Art Director: Jeff Batzli
Designers: Jennifer Markson, Midori Nakamura, and Wendy Fields
Color Illustrations: Susan Kemnitz
Blueprint Illustrations: Kirsten Berger
Photography Editor: Paquita Bass

Color separations by Bright Arts Pte Ltd.
Printed in China by Leefung-Asco Printers Ltd.

1 3 5 7 9 10 8 6 4 2

For bulk purchases and special sales, please contact:
Michael Friedman Publishing Group, Inc.
Attention: Sales Department
230 Fifth Avenue
New York, NY 10001
212/685-6610 FAX 212/685-3916

Visit our website:
www.metrobooks.com

Dedication

In loving tribute to my mother, Elizabeth Turner Price, who died before this book was completed.
I treasure my memories of watching her tending lush pots of flowers on the deck.

Contents

How to Use This Book **9**

Things You Need to Know **10**

What You Will Need **17**

A Formal Entry Garden **18**

　　You Will Need…

　　Plant List and Garden Plan

　　Planting the Formal Entry Garden, Step by Step

　　Calendar of Care

　　Getting to Know the Plants

A Moon Garden **28**

　　You Will Need…

　　Plant List and Garden Plan

　　Planting the Moon Garden, Step by Step

　　Calendar of Care

　　Getting to Know the Plants

A Hummingbird and Butterfly Garden **38**

　　You Will Need…

　　Plant List and Garden Plan

　　Planting the Hummingbird and Butterfly Garden, Step by Step

　　Calendar of Care

　　Getting to Know the Plants

A Children's Vegetable Garden **48**

　　You Will Need…

　　Plant List and Garden Plan

　　Planting the Children's Vegetable Garden, Step by Step

　　Calendar of Care

　　Getting to Know the Plants

A Half-Barrel Water Garden **64**

　　You Will Need…

　　Plant List and Garden Plan

　　Planting the Half-Barrel Water Garden, Step by Step

　　Calendar of Care

　　Getting to Know the Plants

Contents

A Garden of Kitchen Herbs . . . .**.74**

You Will Need...

Plant List and Garden Plan

Planting the Garden of Kitchen Herbs, Step by Step

Calendar of Care

Getting to Know the Plants

A Fragrant Garden . . . .**.86**

You Will Need...

Plant List and Garden Plan

Planting the Fragrant Garden, Step by Step

Calendar of Care

Getting to Know the Plants

A Hot Color Garden . . . .**.98**

You Will Need...

Plant List and Garden Plan

Planting the Hot Color Garden, Step by Step

Calendar of Care

Getting to Know the Plants

A Shady Garden **110**

You Will Need...

Plant List and Garden Plan

Planting the Shady Garden, Step by Step

Calendar of Care

Getting to Know the Plants

A Window Box Garden **124**

You Will Need...

Plant List and Garden Plan

Planting the Window Box Garden, Step by Step

Calendar of Care

Getting to Know the Plants

Plant Hardiness Zones **134**

Appendix **135**

Index **142**

How to Use This Book

Planting in containers is perhaps the easiest way of all to begin gardening. The investment of time and money is minimal, and the pleasure to be had from pots filled to overflowing with colorful, scented blooms is more than worth the effort. Container gardening is also a perfect solution for people with limited space and those with minimal time to care for a garden.

This book is designed to walk you step by step through the process of planning and planting a beautiful, easy-to-maintain container garden. Ten different theme gardens offer wonderful choices for different garden types—one of which is bound to catch your fancy. Each garden plan contains a detailed blueprint plus close-up portraits that describe the plants featured in the design. For each garden discussed, you'll find basic "how-to" information on planting, plus lists of necessary tools and equipment. Special boxes give good advice on plant substitutions, garden accents, and other details that might be useful to beginning gardeners, while a calendar of care points out the necessary maintenance for each season. There are also suggestions for ways to customize these plans to suit your particular landscape needs.

Flip through the pages to familiarize yourself with the plans and plants, then pick a garden plan that you like. Before buying a single pot or flower (or even driving to the garden center), make sure to read "Things You Need to Know" beginning on page 10. This will give you the basics you'll need to get started. Next, read through all the information contained for the garden plan you've chosen. Some of the questions you have—"How often do I have to water the pots?" or "What do I do with my container garden when winter comes?"—will be answered as you read. Refer back to Things You Need to Know as you plan and plant; while each garden design section explains the steps you need to take to plan, install, and care for your container garden, the general introduction provides information in greater detail about such topics as good soil mixes and proper watering practices.

Note that some of the plans are very straightforward, using only a few types of plants, while others are a bit more involved. Whichever plan you choose, you are only a few simple steps away from a beautiful, healthy garden just outside your window.

THINGS YOU NEED TO KNOW

1. CHOOSING A SOIL MIX

There are many good commercial potting mixes available in garden centers and general purpose stores. Most of these mixes are various combinations of peat, vermiculite, perlite, sand, and soil, and nearly any basic commercial mix will provide a sufficient growing medium for the plants suggested in this book. If you'd like to make your own potting mix, combine two parts peat, one part vermiculite, and

one part coarse sand (all purchased by the bag, as these ingredients are sterilized to make them appropriate for container use). One thing you should certainly not do is dig soil from your backyard and use it in your pots. Not only is this soil too heavy for most container plants to thrive in, it can also harbor soil-dwelling insects, diseases, or toxins.

2. FINDING AN APPROPRIATE CONTAINER

There are probably as many shapes, sizes, and styles of containers as there are different types of plants. Some of the garden plans in this book suggest a particular type of container, but you are always free to follow your own preference, keeping in mind a few important points: the pot must have adequate drainage holes, it must be the right size for the plants it will hold, and it must be of a safe weight for the spot it will occupy. Large, heavy planters filled with potting soil and plants may jeopardize the structural integrity of a roof, deck, porch, or balcony, and even if the roof or other structure is very sturdy, heavier containers are best placed where structural supports are located. If you have any doubts about the weight-bearing capacity of the structure where your container garden will be sited, check with a licensed landscape or building contractor before proceeding. Indeed, avoid placing large stone and cement planters on a structure at all, reserving them instead for solid patios, terraces, or walkways.

Following are materials that make good containers for plants: terra-cotta (plain or glazed), ceramic, stone, reconstituted stone (a material made from stone ground into particles, liquefied, and poured into molds), metal, cement (a mix of powdered stone, clay, resins, and aggregates), and wood. On the market today are also lightweight planters made of fiberglass, plastic, Styrofoam, and other modern materials that mimic the look of traditional stone, metal, or terra-cotta.

Note that many containers are made from materials that may crack if left outdoors in cold winter weather—cement, stone, terra-cotta, and ceramic can all be vulnerable—so if you have no storage space for your containers or simply don't want to move them, choose those that are advertised to be weatherproof. If you elect to move them indoors for the winter, remember that weight may be a factor, and purchase ones that can be moved easily or install them on wheeled bases.

3. Planting the Containers

First, select a pot large enough for the eventual size of your plants (see "Getting to Know the Plants" for the garden plan you have chosen); a good rule of thumb is that the height of the plant should be no more than $1\frac{1}{2}$ times the height of the container. In most cases, your pots will feature more than one plant, and in this case you should use the tallest plant in the group as your guide. If the pot has been used before, make sure it is clean; if it needs to be cleaned, use a solution of nine parts water to one part bleach.

First, add a layer of drainage material to the bottom of the pot—broken crockery and stones are excellent choices. Chips of Styrofoam or packing peanuts (but not the water soluble or biodegradable kind) will also work, and are lighter than rocks or shards of crockery. Next, fill the container a little more than three-quarters full with your chosen potting mix.

Beginning with the largest plant, remove the plants from their containers by laying the container on its side and rolling it back and forth gently to loosen the soil and roots (see the next step if you are planting a tree or shrub). Lift the plant carefully by the base of the stem and pull it from the container, inspecting the roots to make sure they

then add more potting mix if necessary. Do be careful, though, not to fill the container all the way to the top, or it will overflow when you water it.

When you are planting a very large container, you can also treat the surface more like a planting bed by filling the container with soil and excavating planting holes with a small spade, trowel, or dibble (a small hand implement for planting bulbs).

The same basic process outlined above can be used to repot plants that seem to be outgrowing their containers.

4. If the Container Will House an Ornamental Tree or a Shrub

Not all trees and shrubs will live happily in containers, but some, including those suggested in this book, will thrive, and can effectively anchor a container garden. If you are deciding to substitute for a tree or shrub in the plan, make sure to look for a dwarf variety or ask an experienced gardener to recommend a shrub that is suited to container life.

If your pot will contain an ornamental tree or shrub, this should be planted first. The shrub should be planted so that the soil is at the same level around the trunk that it

are not tightly packed and wound around themselves. If they are, simply use a sharp knife to cut down the side of the root mass and tease the roots apart with your fingers. Then set the plant on the soil according to the layout of the garden blueprint you've chosen, making design adjustments as you go if you need to.

Once you have finished arranging the plants, begin to install them one by one. Using a trowel, make a hole large enough to accommodate the plant's roots and set the plant in the hole. Fill in around the roots of the plants with potting mix, and press gently on the soil. Water thoroughly, was in its original container (typically, you can see a mark on the trunk to show where the soil level was). To remove a tree or shrub from a nursery container, lay it on its side and gently roll the container back and forth to loosen the soil. With one hand on the trunk and one hand on the base of the container, carefully extract the plant from the container. The roots should not be tightly packed or growing out through the hole in the container bottom.

Set the tree or shrub in the container on top of the soil layer. You may want a helper to stand back and tell you if the tree or shrub is planted straight. Decide which part of the plant you want to face forward, too, in case one side looks better than another. Once the plant is level, straight, and centered in the container, start filling in around the sides of the shrub with additional soil, just until the tree is supported (unless it is the only plant to occupy the container). It may be helpful to have a friend support the tree while you add the rest of the plants.

Being careful not to disturb the tree's roots too much, add the other plants to the container. Fill in with additional soil (again, be sure not to exceed the depth to which the tree or shrub was originally planted), then tamp the soil down gently and water well.

5. PLANTING SEEDS

In the following plans I recommend some plants that you may like to start from seed. This is by far the least expensive way to grow plants, so if you are willing to wait a bit for them to grow, try your hand at sowing seeds (you can always purchase flats if you prefer). Where seeds are indicated, they can be planted directly in the soil of the container. Use a hand-held garden fork to make shallow furrows in the soil, then sprinkle the seeds as evenly as possible into the furrows. Smooth over the soil with your hands to cover the seeds, then water, using a gentle spray hose attachment to prevent the stream of water from washing the seeds away.

When the seedlings come up, thin them by pulling out about half of them (I know, it's hard!). The rest of the seedlings will now have their best chance of survival.

6. FEEDING YOUR CONTAINER PLANTS

Plants in containers generally require more fertilizing than those in the ground, because they quickly absorb the nutrients in their limited plot of soil. After your plants have become established (usually a few weeks), you can begin feeding them with a commercial fertilizer that is well-balanced and contains nitrogen, phosphorus, potassium, and trace elements. Fertilizers are commonly sold at garden centers, hardware stores, and general purpose stores. It's best to err on the side of caution, since too much fertilizer can burn plant roots and even kill the plant, so be sure to follow label directions carefully. Or, to be on the safe side, use the fertilizer at half the strength recommended on the label every ten days to two weeks.

7. WATERING YOUR PLANTS

A container can dry out quickly because the overall volume of the soil is relatively small, and thus vulnerable to evaporation. Rain may help, but don't count on the weather alone to supply enough moisture for your potted plants. To tell if your containers need water, stick your finger an inch or two into the soil and see if it is dry. If it is, your plants need water. In hot summer weather, unless you have rain, you will most likely need to water your garden every day.

If possible, water in the morning, before the sun is strong enough to evaporate the water quickly, and try to use water that is neither very cold nor very hot. If you must water in the evening when you get home from work, make sure that the drainage is excellent (the layer of crockery or gravel added to the bottom of the pot should be extensive). This will help prevent the roots from sitting in water at night, which can lead to disease.

8. PRUNING AND DEADHEADING

Pruning can be fairly complicated, but here we will reduce it to its most basic elements. Sometimes you may prune to improve the shape of the tree or shrub or encourage new growth and flowering, while at other times you may prune to get rid of crossed, damaged, or diseased branches. Any plants for which pruning is recommended, but which should be treated differently from these guidelines, are noted in the garden plan.

First, always use clean, sharp pruners, shears, or loppers, using rubbing alcohol to wipe the blade after each pruning cut from a diseased tree or shrub. Remove any dead, dying, damaged, or weak branches with a clean, angled cut at the point where the branch is attached to the parent stem.

If you are shaping the shrub or tree, prune it back to just above a bud or an intersecting branch. Most shrubs that bloom in spring can be safely pruned after they have flowered.

Deadheading, on the other hand, refers to the practice of snipping off the heads of flowers that have faded. This not only removes the sometimes unsightly dead blooms, it often encourages a repeat bloom because the plant does not need to put its energy into producing the seeds that would normally follow the flower.

9. THE DIFFERENCE BETWEEN ANNUALS AND PERENNIALS

An annual grows from seed, flowers, and produces seeds all in one year. It then dies and must be replaced unless it is self-seeding, that is, unless it scatters its seeds, which come up the next year. Annuals are often thought of as "cheap and cheerful"; they add color and grow quickly, filling in gaps that might exist in the garden until slower-growing perennials are well-established. They also tend to have a long period of bloom, an attractive quality in a garden plant.

Perennials live more than two years; their roots survive over the winter (unless the plant is grown outside its hardiness zone [see number 10]), and the plant returns year after year. Some perennials survive indefinitely given the right conditions, while others last only four or five years. There are also biennials, which come to maturity over two seasons and then die, and bulbs, which typically reappear for years before becoming exhausted and dying.

10. FIGURING OUT YOUR PLANT HARDINESS ZONE

Plant hardiness zones indicate whether a plant is ideally suited for the average weather conditions in a particular climate. The zones provide guidelines for which plants will survive in which regions, but are not guarantees that a plant will make it through a particularly severe winter or a scorching summer, and the particular conditions in each garden will also affect a plant's performance. Consult the map on page 134 to determine your hardiness zone, and then check the zones listed in the "Getting to Know the Plants"

section of the plan you have chosen to make sure that the plants are suited for your area. Most of the plants in these plans have been chosen for their reliability in a wide array of regions. Note that annuals often do not have a plant hardiness zone (or read "All Zones"), because these assignments are based on whether or not the plant will survive the winter. Since annuals will die after one growing season, they may not be assigned a hardiness zone.

11. Winter Care

All container gardens need some preparation for the winter, though the amount of care they need is in proportion to the severity of the winter weather in your area. After a killing frost, pull up the annuals in the containers and discard or compost them. If the pot held only annuals, discard the soil, clean the pot, and store it indoors for the winter.

Trees, shrubs, and perennials planted in tubs are more vulnerable than those in the ground, where the soil's temperature is more even and changes are gradual. In cold climates (where the temperatures reach freezing), your permanent pots and containers will most likely need some protection from the elements. If the planter cannot be moved, apply a thick layer of mulch and a blanket of evergreen branches over the soil to protect plants from freeze and thaw cycles. Containers that can be moved are best transferred to a garage, shed, or unheated porch, where they will be somewhat sheltered. Pots on a terrace, patio, or rooftop will fare best if they are grouped close together in a corner, up against a sheltering wall. Bales of hay or plastic bags filled with dry leaves nestled around the pots will provide further protection.

WHAT YOU WILL NEED

You will need some basic tools to begin your container garden and care for it properly. There are also some optional tools that are nice to have on hand, but not absolutely essential. If you have neighbors who like to garden, you might consider a tool-sharing arrangement to cut down on the purchase of tools you won't need very often.

The Essentials

- A set of trowels for digging holes and scooping soil and mulch; you will need both a narrow, pointed style and one with a rounded end
- A small spade, useful for filling large containers
- A hand rake, for weeding large pots and loosening soil in containers
- A dibble (a small hand implement) to make holes for planting bulbs and large seeds
- All-purpose pruners

- A sharp garden knife
- Loppers, for cutting branches more than $1/2$ inch in diameter
- A watering can, with a rose head for delicate seedlings; the long-spouted ones are good for reaching hanging baskets and containers at the back of a grouping
- A hose with an adjustable nozzle (unless you have a very small grouping)
- A broom

Optional Tools and Equipment

- A pair of floral snips, for deadheading
- A pair of good garden gloves
- Plant supports, if you will be growing plants that need staking (see individual plans)
- Twine or garden ties for tying plants to stakes

A FORMAL ENTRY GARDEN

Whether your home is an imposing brick townhouse, a center-hall colonial, or a quaint Victorian, the entryway is one of its most important features. A grouping of potted plants clustered at the front door, marching up the steps, or arranged along a walkway create a welcoming vignette. The following design presents a sophisticated approach to an entryway, whether you choose to plant the eye-catching standard roses or the all-evergreen alternative. By incorporating evergreen shrubs, the plantings provide year-round interest, much the way traditional foundation plantings do. Evergreen topiaries require a bit more upkeep than most annuals or perennials, as they need to be carefully and regularly shaped. Alas, unlike shrubs planted in the ground, evergreens in pots may fail to thrive after several seasons. By selecting dwarf varieties and by paying close attention to watering and fertilizing schedules, you may prolong the life of pot-grown evergreen shrubs.

PLANTING THE FORMAL ENTRY GARDEN, STEP BY STEP

Step 1: Begin with a clean container, either an urn or a Versailles box (a square, wooden planter). Layer drainage material—shards of crockery, gravel, or Styrofoam peanuts—in the bottom of the container, then fill about halfway with potting mix (set the containerized rose in the container on top of the soil to check proper depth; the top of the soil in the nursery container should be about 2 or 3 inches below the lip of the new container).

Step 2: Before planting the rose, drive the support stake into the soil next to the spot for the rose. Remove the rose from the nursery container by tipping it on its side and tapping it to release the plant. Tease the roots apart if they appear tightly packed. Grasping the rootball, set the plant on the soil beside the stake, and fill in with additional soil around the roots. Tie the trunk to the stake with tree-ties. Water well. Prune the strongest rose canes back to 6 to 8 inches after you've planted it.

Step 3: Plant the alyssum seeds in the soil around the rose, covering only lightly with soil, as sun stimulates germination. If you have started seeds early or purchased

YOU WILL NEED...

- 2 large containers for the roses and 6 smaller ones for the boxwood topiaries

- Broken terra-cotta pieces, gravel, or Styrofoam peanuts for drainage

- Potting soil

- A small spade, for filling the containers

- A trowel, for digging holes and filling in soil around the plants

- Sharp pruning shears

- 2 bamboo support stakes (the stakes should be at least a foot taller than the trunk of the rose)

- Tree-ties (or sturdy, rubber-coated wire)

PLANT LIST

1. Standard rose (*Rosa* spp.)

2. Alyssum (*Lobularia maritima*)

3. Boxwood topiary (*Buxus* spp.)

4. Variegated ivy (*Hedera* spp.)

A FORMAL ENTRY GARDEN

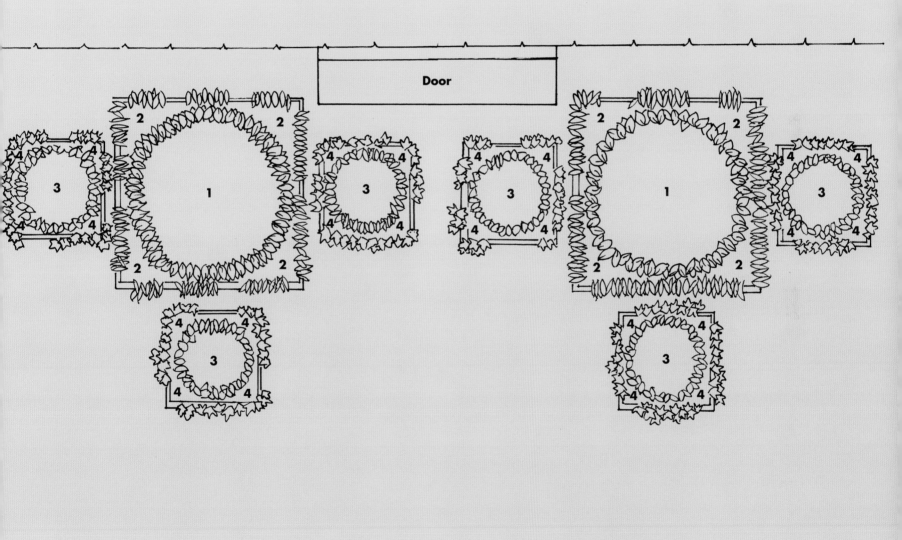

Door

*This plan has been condensed to fit on the page. Leave ample space between the two pot groupings as a path to the door.

flats, plant the seedlings in the container, making sure not to disturb the roots of the rose.

Step 4: Next, plant the six boxwood topiaries. Place drainage material and soil in the containers, to about halfway. One by one, remove the shrubs from their containers, place them on the soil, and fill in with additional soil. Never install plants deeper than they were planted at the nursery. You can usually see a mark on the trunk to show where the soil level was.

Step 5: Being careful of the roots of the newly planted boxwood, dig small holes with a hand trowel, and plant the variegated ivy. Once all have been planted, water well.

EVERGREEN VARIATION

If you want a planting that will look good all year long, consider replacing the standard roses in this plan with evergreen topiaries that complement the boxwood spheres. Alberta spruce, San Jose holly, and juniper are all good possibilities, and these may be cut into a cone or a spiral (note that the more complicated the form, the more difficult it will be to maintain, and you may need to call upon a professional gardener to help with this on a twice-yearly basis). At Christmas time, weave tiny white fairy lights throughout the shrubs and tie miniature red bows to the branches.

CALENDAR OF CARE

SPRING: *Plant the container garden after all danger of frost in your area has passed. After the first year, prune the roses in spring, cutting the previous year's growth back to about 8 inches long. Prune out any diseased or crossed branches, shaping the "tree" as you go. Look over the boxwood topiaries and prune back any dead shoots.*

SUMMER: *Water containers daily in the heat of summer, and fertilize the rose/alyssum container every two weeks. The boxwood container needs less fertilizing, about once a month. Deadhead the roses and annuals to promote additional flowering. With small, sharp shears, trim boxwood topiaries to maintain their round, compact forms; keep the plants well trimmed for maximum formality.*

AUTUMN: *In early autumn, prune back several inches of the roses' growth, including new growth. Before frost, remove the variegated ivy from the containers and repot it to use the following year. Keep it indoors throughout the winter. Once the alyssum has been killed by frost, pull it up and discard or compost.*

WINTER: *If you have planted standard roses, move them to a frost-free environment such as an unheated shed or enclosed porch for the winter, as the trunks are vulnerable to damage. If you don't have a spot for them, move them against a sheltered wall, wrap the trunks in horticultural fleece, and nestle bags filled with dry leaves around the pots. Mulch the boxwood or other evergreen containers and add a layer of evergreen branches to blanket the soil. If you intend to leave the containers out all winter, be sure to purchase weather-resistant ones.*

GETTING TO KNOW THE PLANTS

'POPCORN' STANDARD ROSE

1. STANDARD ROSE   (*Rosa* spp.)

CLASSIFICATION: Shrub rose

PLANT HARDINESS ZONES: 6 to 9, with winter protection

ULTIMATE SIZE: 2'–6' tall

BLOOM TIME: Summer

SUN REQUIREMENT: Full sun

Standard roses, also called tree roses, are excellent for container culture, and give a highly formal appearance with a relative minimum of upkeep. These are actually roses that have been grafted high onto the trunk of a rugosa rose. As standard roses may become top-heavy with new growth, it is important to prune the rose back in spring and autumn as described in the Calendar of Care. Winter care depends very much on the region in which you live, but standard roses are quite tender. It is best to move the roses to a protected spot, such as an unheated garage, shed, or screened porch.

ROSES AREN'T THE ONLY STANDARDS

If you prefer the look of another flower, there are several good candidates for this type of treatment. Try one of these others as a standard:

Hibiscus (*Hibiscus* spp.)

Fuchsia (*Fuchsia* spp.)

Marguerite daisies
(*Chrysanthemum frutescens*)

ALYSSUM

2. **ALYSSUM** (*Lobularia maritima*)

CLASSIFICATION: Annual
PLANT HARDINESS ZONES: All zones
ULTIMATE SIZE: 4"–8" tall and 6" wide
BLOOM TIME: Late spring to autumn
SUN REQUIREMENT: Full sun to partial shade

Flowers of this popular edging plant may be white, pink, or purple. One of the reasons it is so coveted is, no doubt, its easy care. Sow seeds directly into the soil once all chance of frost has passed, or plant seeds indoors 6 to 8 weeks before you intend to plant outdoors. You can also purchase alyssum in flats. Deadhead to promote further flowering.

BOXWOOD TOPIARY

3. BOXWOOD TOPIARY
(*Buxus* spp.)

CLASSIFICATION: Evergreen shrub
PLANT HARDINESS ZONES: 5 to 9
ULTIMATE SIZE: To 5' tall and wide
BLOOM TIME: None
SUN REQUIREMENT: Full sun to
partial shade

Look for a dwarf boxwood—*Buxus spempervirens* 'Suffruticosa' is a good one. Dwarf boxwood has the advantage of remaining naturally small, so will be well suited to your pots. It will need to be trimmed to maintain its compact, rounded form. Mist it over the first summer, until it is well established, if the weather is hot and dry. This is a classic evergreen topiary plant, due in part to its very dense foliage.

'GLOIRE DE MARENGO' VARIEGATED IVY

4. VARIEGATED IVY   (*Hedera* spp.)

CLASSIFICATION: Perennial
PLANT HARDINESS ZONES: All zones if wintered indoors; 8 to 10 outdoors
ULTIMATE SIZE: 6"–12" tall and spreading
BLOOM TIME: None
SUN REQUIREMENT: Partial shade

Variegated ivies are somewhat less hardy than the straight green species, but all are easy to care for. Ivy can be found at garden centers and nurseries in small containers; you can propagate additional plants from cuttings. At the end of the growing season, cut several tendrils from the plants and root them in water or moist sand. Keep them indoors, and you should have viable plants in about a year. In cold climates, remove ivy before a killing frost and repot it. Bring the plant indoors for the winter, and reuse it the following spring.

A MOON GARDEN

Gardeners have long had a fascination with pure white flowers. In the 1930s, legendary gardener Vita Sackville-West installed an all-white garden at Sissinghurst, one of England's most celebrated estates, where the garden continues to delight millions of visitors. Here, I've interpreted the all-white garden for a container grouping, meant to be enjoyed on moonlit evenings. The abundance of white blooms in this garden will seem to shimmer and glow in the soft light of evening, though the garden is certainly no less attractive at other times of day. The heliotrope is heavily fragrant, stimulating the sense of smell, which becomes even sharper at night.

The potted garden outlined in this plan incorporates easy-to-grow plants with white blooms and with silver and variegated foliage that reinforce and accentuate the white theme. A vine trained up a tripod adds structure and height to this charming vignette.

This garden can be planted in spring, after the last frost date, and is best sited in a sunny spot, with some protection from the sun's rays during the afternoon (this is mainly for the variegated ivy, which prefers a bit of shade). Keep in mind that many of these plants are annuals, which do not mind a bit of crowding.

PLANTING THE MOON GARDEN, STEP BY STEP

Step 1: Begin with the largest pot, which will hold the moonflower and an underplanting of helichrysum. First, add a layer of drainage material, either broken crockery, gravel, or 2 inches worth of Styrofoam peanuts, then fill the container with potting soil to within about 2 inches of the top. Set the bamboo stakes into the soil at even intervals along the edge of the container, and tie tops together with twine.

Step 2: Moonflower seeds are best sown directly into the soil, after all danger of frost has passed. Soak the seeds overnight in tepid water; once the seeds are finished soaking, nick the seed coatings with a sharp knife, then insert them $1/2$ inch into the soil. Place several seeds at the center of the pot and two or three at the base of each stake. You can thin the seedlings once they have germinated.

Step 3: Remove the helichrysum from their containers and tease the roots apart with your fingers. Place 2 or 3 helichrysum at even intervals around the edge of the container. Water thoroughly and add more soil as needed.

YOU WILL NEED...

- Several containers of various sizes, each with drainage holes (7 pots, if you plant according to the plan outlined here)

- Three 5- to 6-foot bamboo stakes (for the tripod)

- Garden twine

- Broken terra-cotta pot pieces, gravel, or Styrofoam peanuts for drainage

- Potting soil, commercial or homemade

- A trowel

PLANT LIST

1. Moonflower (*Ipomea alba*)

2. 'All Triumph' dahlia (*Dahlia* 'All Triumph')

3. Heliotrope (*Heliotropium* spp.)

4. 'Apple Blossom' flowering tobacco (*Nicotiana* 'Apple Blossom')

5. Helichrysum (*Helichrysum petiolare* 'Variegatum')

6. Petunia (*Petunia* x *hybrida*)

7. Variegated ivy (*Hedera* spp.)

A MOON GARDEN

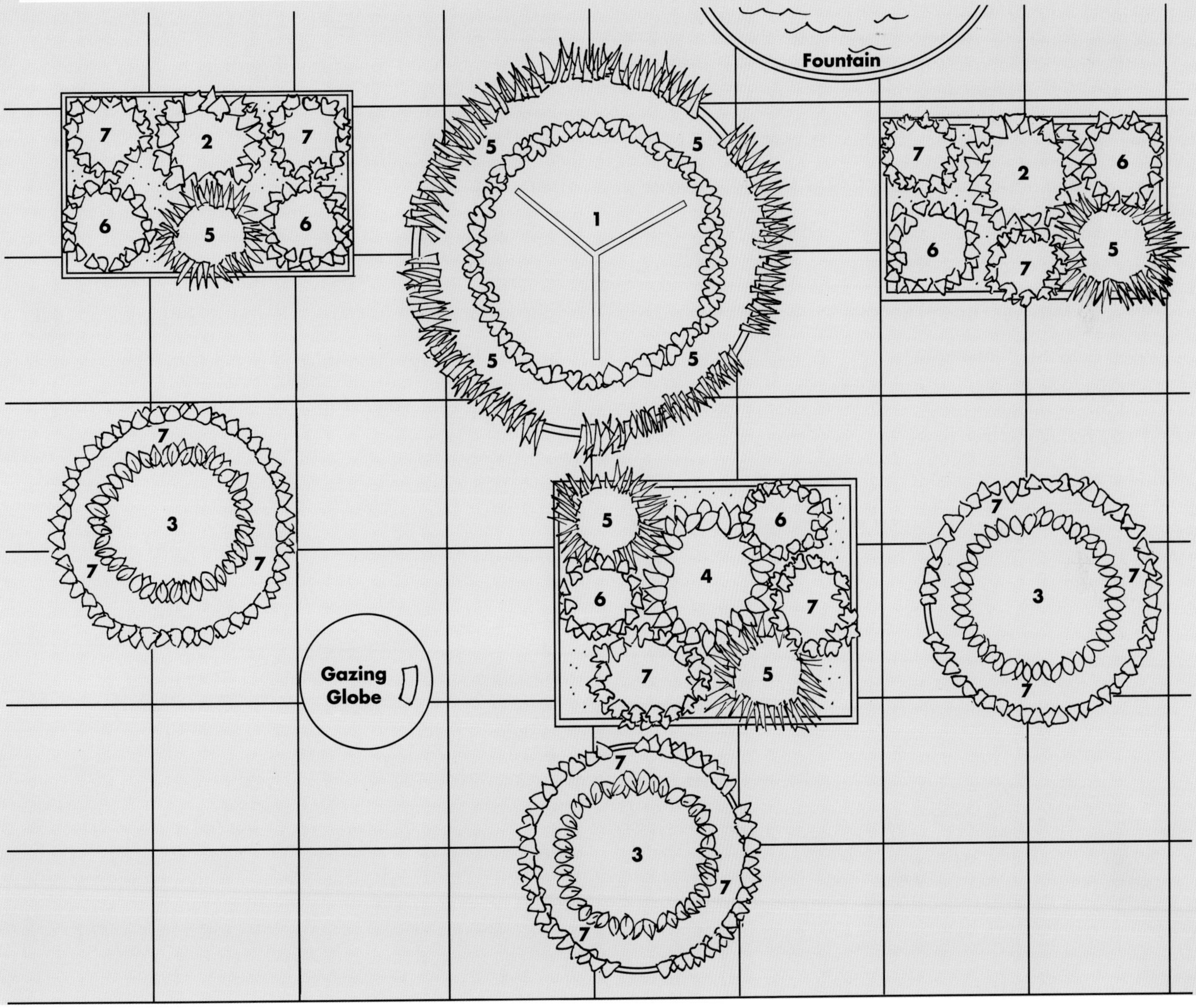

Fountain

7 2 7
6 5 6

5 1 5
5 5

7
3
7 7

5 6
6 4 7
7 5

7 2 6
6 7 5

7
3
7 7

Gazing
Globe

7
3
7 7

Step 4: Next, plant the dahlia containers. Prepare the pot with drainage material and potting soil as described in Step 1. Remove the plants—the dahlias, helichrysum, petunias, and variegated ivy—from their containers and place as indicated by the garden design blueprint. (If you are planting dahlia tubers instead of seedlings, lay them in the soil horizontally; they should be planted 3 inches deep from their bases.) Feel free to move the plants around a bit until they look good to you. Fill in gaps with additional potting soil, pressing down firmly with fingers or with trowel handle. Water thoroughly and add more soil as needed.

Step 5: Plant the flowering tobacco grouping—the flowering tobacco, helichrysum, variegated ivy, and petunias—following the same process as used for the other containers, again watering thoroughly when you are finished. The flowering tobacco is best started from seed, 6 to 8 weeks before you intend to plant outdoors. (Sow them on top of a flat of potting mix, only lightly covered, as light speeds their germination).

Step 6: Finally, plant the heliotrope pots. The heliotrope can easily be started as seeds, 10 weeks before you intend to plant outdoors. These pots are the smallest of the garden, and probably only require 1 heliotrope and 3 petunias per pot. Prepare the container with drainage material and potting soil, then plant as previously described and water well.

CALENDAR OF CARE

SPRING: *If you are starting any of your plants from seed, plant them 6 to 12 weeks before the last predicted frost (follow the instructions on the seed packets). Otherwise, you can simply purchase most of the plants in flats and plant this container garden outdoors after the last predicted frost date.*

SUMMER: *Water every day in hot, dry weather. Fertilize every 3 weeks, according to directions on the product label. Deadhead annuals to maximize bloom (see "Things You Need to Know" to review). As the moonflower vine grows, train its tendrils up the bamboo tripod by twining them around the poles. In midsummer, cut the petunias back to stimulate new, thicker growth.*

AUTUMN: *In cold climates (zones 8 and north), remove ivy before a killing frost and repot. Bring it indoors or into a greenhouse. As the estimated first frost date draws near, dig up the dahlia tubers, set in a cool, dry place and allow to dry. Remove spent foliage and stems. Store dried tubers in peat moss, saw dust, or shredded newspaper in a cool, dry place. Some people choose to treat dahlias like annuals, and simply start over with new ones the following year. Discard or compost other annuals after a killing frost.*

WINTER: *In cold climates, store any pots or containers subject to cracking and weather damage indoors or in a protected place such as an attached garage.*

GETTING TO KNOW THE PLANTS

MOONFLOWER

1. MOONFLOWER (*Ipomea alba*)

CLASSIFICATION: Annual vine (perennial in tropical climates)
PLANT HARDINESS ZONES: All zones
ULTIMATE SIZE: 8'–10' tall
BLOOM TIME: Midsummer til frost
SUN REQUIREMENT: Full sun

The fragrant, satiny, white, 5-inch blooms of this morning glory relative begin flowering in the evening and stay open until the morning sun begins to shine directly on them. This vine thrives in hot weather, and is slow to start until the temperature is consistently above 70 degrees. Once started, the moonflower blooms abundantly, with each flower lasting only one night, but new ones coming into flower continuously. Moonflowers are easy to grow, and while you can certainly buy seedlings, it is very simple to start the seeds yourself. Simply presoak and score the seeds before planting.

2. 'ALL TRIUMPH' DAHLIA (*Dahlia* 'All Triumph')

CLASSIFICATION: Bulb (tuber)
PLANT HARDINESS ZONES: All zones
   (8 to 10 for overwintering)
ULTIMATE SIZE: 1'–2' tall and 6" wide
BLOOM TIME: Summer til frost
SUN REQUIREMENT: Full sun

'All Triumph' is a neat, pure white, low-growing cultivar perfect for containers. Its petals are "semi-cactus" shaped, which means that they are flat at the base and rolled near the tips. You can also select another white dahlia cultivar. Native to Mexico, dahlias are tender and will not overwinter in the ground above Zone 8, but you can lift them and store them indoors, to be replanted the next season.

'ALL TRIUMPH' DAHLIA

'WHITE LADY' HELIOTROPE

3. HELIOTROPE

(*Heliotropium* spp.)

CLASSIFICATION: Annual
   (perennial in warm climates)
PLANT HARDINESS ZONES: All zones as
   annual
ULTIMATE SIZE: 1' tall and wide
BLOOM TIME: Summer to autumn
SUN REQUIREMENT: Full sun

This bushy, free-flowering plant bears clusters of small blooms in white or shades of purple. A favorite of butterflies, the flowers are heavily fragrant, with a scent reminiscent of vanilla. This plant likes lots of sun and water, and should be fertilized regularly. If you are starting from seed, sow the seeds in sandy soil about 10 weeks before outdoor planting.

4. FLOWERING TOBACCO

(*Nicotiana* 'Apple Blossom')

CLASSIFICATION: Annual
PLANT HARDINESS ZONES: All zones
ULTIMATE SIZE: 12"–15" tall
BLOOM TIME: Early summer til frost
SUN REQUIREMENT: Full sun to partial shade

There are many worthy cultivars of old-fashioned flowering tobacco, and this is only one—experiment with others if you like. 'Apple Blossom' was chosen for its color: white blushed with pink. Flowering tobacco is beautifully fragranced and bears star-shaped blooms available in a variety of colors, from red to pink to white to lime green. Heat- and cold-tolerant, this popular flower is incredibly easygoing. Start seeds 4 to 6 weeks before you plan to plant them outdoors.

'APPLE BLOSSOM' FLOWERING TOBACCO

'VARIEGATUM' VARIEGATED HELICHRYSUM

5. VARIEGATED HELICHRYSUM

(*Helichrysum petiolare* 'Variegatum')

CLASSIFICATION: Annual, perennial in warm climates

PLANT HARDINESS ZONES: All zones as annual

ULTIMATE SIZE: 8"–10" (trailing) and 12" wide

BLOOM TIME: Grown for foliage

SUN REQUIREMENT: Sun to partial shade

Also called licorice plant, variegated helichrysum has beautiful lime green leaves with silver mottling. The velvety leaf texture, too, provides interest. Helichrysum's trailing habit and downy green leaves make it the perfect foil for a container planting, where it fills in and complements, without distracting from, the "stars" of the show.

GOOD ACCENTS FOR THIS GARDEN

Most gardens benefit from interesting accents, which act as focal points and provide additional structure to the space. The following are a few excellent choices to ornament the moon garden:

* A silver gazing ball, to capture interesting reflections

* A series of white paper luminarias (make sure they are always attended, due to risk of fire)

* A small bubbling fountain, for its soothing sounds

6. PETUNIA *(Petunia x hybrida)*

CLASSIFICATION: Annual
PLANT HARDINESS ZONES: All zones
ULTIMATE SIZE: To 12" tall and 8"–12" spread
BLOOM TIME: Early summer to autumn
SUN REQUIREMENT: Full sun to partial shade

Petunias are garden favorites, and are particularly useful in containers. New, trailing varieties are especially lovely, as their free-blooming branches cascade over the tops of the pots. Choose a white variety for your moon garden. Sow the seeds indoors 6 to 8 weeks before planting outdoors or buy them in flats from your favorite garden center. In midsummer, petunias benefit from being cut back, especially if they've begun to look a bit straggly.

PETUNIA

'VARIEGATA' VARIEGATED IVY

7. VARIEGATED IVY *(Hedera spp.)*

CLASSIFICATION: Perennial
PLANT HARDINESS ZONES: All zones if wintered indoors; 8 to 10 outdoors
ULTIMATE SIZE: 6"–12" tall and spreading
BLOOM TIME: None
SUN REQUIREMENT: Partial shade

Ivy requires minimal care and contributes soothing greens to containers. Variegated types, of which there are many, tend to be less hardy than their all-green cousins. You can purchase ivy in small containers for the first season, and can easily create more by taking cuttings. Simply snip a few pieces from the plants at the end of the garden season and root them in water or moist sand and set on a windowsill. A new, viable plant will be ready for a display container in about a year. In cold climates, remove ivy before a killing frost and repot it. Bring the plant indoors for the winter, and reuse it the following spring.

A HUMMINGBIRD AND BUTTERFLY GARDEN

Few visitors are more welcome to our gardens than hummingbirds and butterflies. As they dance among the flowers, seeking nourishment, they invariably impart a sense of serenity and enchantment. And the sight of a tiny, ferocious "hummer" parent chasing away much larger birds to protect its young is both hilarious and awe-inspiring.

Both butterflies and hummingbirds draw nectar from blooms, with hummingbirds in particular attracted to bright red or orange trumpet-shaped flowers. In order to lure them to the pots in your garden, plant some of their favorites and simply wait quietly until they arrive.

It is important to remember that both types of creatures are susceptible to chemical poisoning, so it is best to avoid the use of pesticides as well as herbicides if you are hoping for frequent visits.

The ruby-throated hummingbird is the only species that lives in the eastern part of the United States, while there are several species native to the West. There are dozens of species of butterflies that thrive all over the country; if you are interested in learning more, purchase a good field guide and let your garden bring the butterflies to you.

PLANTING THE HUMMINGBIRD AND BUTTERFLY GARDEN, STEP BY STEP

Step 1: Start with the largest pot, which will hold the butterfly bush and an underplanting of petunias and catmint. Add a layer of drainage material—broken crockery, gravel, or Styrofoam peanuts—to the bottom of the pot, then fill the container with potting soil to about 3 inches below the top. Dig a hole with a trowel or small spade, large enough to accommodate the rootball of the butterfly bush. Remove the shrub from its container by laying it on its side and gently rolling it back and forth to loosen the soil. Set the butterfly bush in the hole and make sure it is straight, then begin filling in with potting soil around the roots.

Plant the petunias and catmint as shown on the garden plan. Be careful not to disturb the roots of the shrub as you install the additional plants. Once the container is planted, water it well.

Step 2: Next, plant the rose mallow container and the fuchsia basket. These plants should be purchased in containers. Simply prepare the next containers with drainage material and soil, remove the plants from their original

YOU WILL NEED...

* 5 pots of various sizes and 1 hanging basket

* Broken crockery, gravel, or Styrofoam peanuts

* Potting soil

* A trowel or small spade

PLANT LIST

1. Butterfly bush (*Buddleia davidii*)

2. Petunias (*Petunia* x *hybrida*)

3. Fuchsia (*Fuchsia* spp.)

4. Salvia (*Salvia* x *splendens*)

5. Zinnias (*Zinnia* spp.)

6. Rose mallow (*Hibiscus moscheutos*)

7. Catmint (*Nepeta* x *faassenii*)

A HUMMINGBIRD AND BUTTERFLY GARDEN

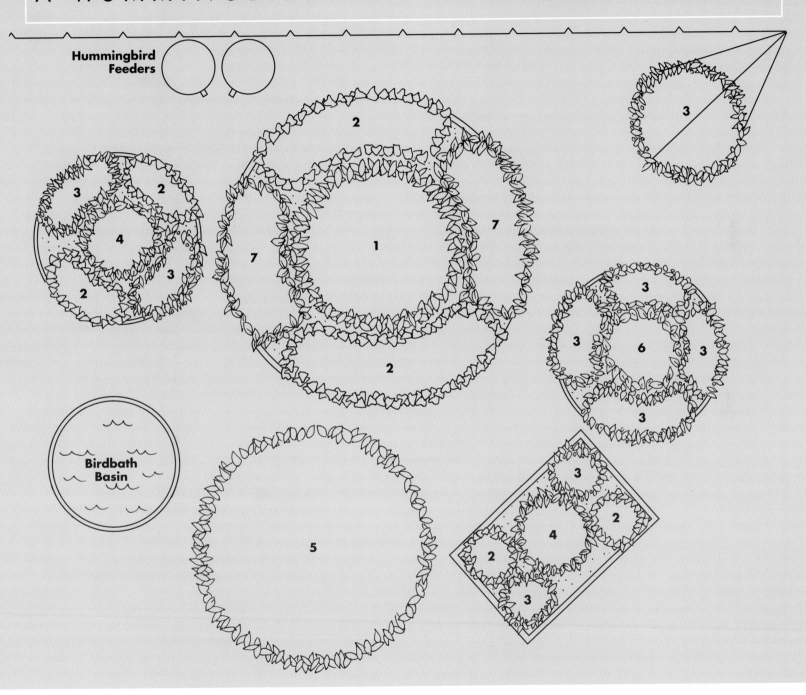

Hummingbird Feeders

Birdbath Basin

containers, and install them. Fill around the plants with soil, pat it firmly, and water well.

Step 3: Plant the zinnias. You can sow seeds directly into the soil in the container after all threat of frost has passed, or you may plant seedlings from zinnias started indoors or flats of seedlings from the nursery. Make sure to space zinnias 12 inches apart to ensure that they get proper air circulation.

Step 4: The final two containers are plantings that feature salvia in combination with petunias and fuchsias. Plant the salvia first at the back of the container, and add one fuchsia to each pot. Fill in with petunias where you have room.

CUTTING BACK A BUTTERFLY BUSH

To ensure maximum bloom, which results in more butterfly visitors, cut the butterfly bush back in early spring. (This shrub blooms on new growth, so it will regrow and bloom in summer.)

Using sharp hand pruners, cut each branch about one foot from the base of the plant at a sharp angle. This angle serves to prevent water from collecting, which could cause rot. Though this kind of hard pruning seems drastic, it is a proven technique for forcing lush new growth.

OTHER BUTTERFLY AND HUMMINGBIRD ATTRACTORS

In addition to the plants in this plan, you can include a few other tried-and-true items to draw ever greater numbers of these winged visitors to your garden. Try one or more of the following:

- A hummingbird feeder, preferably bright red (but never use the colored commercial nectar, as the coloring could be bad for the birds)

- A shallow birdbath or a rock basin filled with water

- A wide, flat rock set in the sun (butterflies like to bask)

CALENDAR OF CARE

SPRING: *Plant the garden in spring after all danger of frost has passed. If you are starting any plants from seed—petunias, salvia, and zinnias are good candidates—plant the seeds indoors 6 to 12 weeks before last frost date (see seed packets for specific instructions). Early the following spring, prune the butterfly bush (see box on page 42). Purchase new butterfly bush and catmint plants as needed.*

Slowly accustom to the outdoors hibiscus and fuchsia plants that have been wintered over indoors. Place them in a sheltered spot out of the wind and direct sunlight and bring them back indoors at night until the weather is predictably warm at night. Remove pots from winter storage and clean thoroughly.

SUMMER: *Water daily in the heat of the summer; the rose mallow, in particular, must be kept moist. Mist the fuchsias, in addition to watering. Deadhead petunias, salvia, and butterfly bush to encourage further flowering. Fertilize every 3 weeks.*

AUTUMN: *Before the first frost, repot rose mallow and fuchsia with fresh potting soil in clean pots before bringing indoors for the winter. Treat with insecticides to avoid infestations.*

After a hard frost, cut back catmint to about 2 inches above soil line. Discard dead annuals. If catmint and butterfly bush are in terra-cotta pots, transfer to plastic pots for the winter. Clean and store pots. In cold climates (zones 7 and above), wrap containers in bubble wrap or in burlap stuffed with dried leaves or straw, or place between stacked bales of hay with open spaces stuffed with dried leaves or straw to protect the root system from freeze and thaw cycles.

WINTER: *Move pots vulnerable to cracking and damage from severe weather to a protected spot, such as a basement or garage, before freezing temperatures arrive.*

GETTING TO KNOW THE PLANTS

'PETITE PLUM' BUTTERFLY BUSH

I. BUTTERFLY BUSH (*Buddleia davidii*)

CLASSIFICATION: Deciduous shrub
PLANT HARDINESS ZONES: 5 to 9
ULTIMATE SIZE: 3'–10' tall and 4'–8' wide
BLOOM TIME: Summer
SUN REQUIREMENT: Full sun to partial shade

True to its name, butterfly bush is adored by these fluttering creatures, and is attractive to hummingbirds as well. Its long clusters of flowers are sweetly fragrant and appear in colors ranging from white to pink to violet. It thrives in well-drained soil and requires regular watering. Deadhead it in the summer to promote further bloom, and prune it back hard in early spring to encourage new growth.

2. PETUNIA (*Petunia* x *hybrida*)

CLASSIFICATION: Annual
PLANT HARDINESS ZONES: All zones
ULTIMATE SIZE: To 12" tall and 8"–12" spread
BLOOM TIME: Early summer to autumn
SUN REQUIREMENT: Full sun to partial shade

Great container plants, petunias are both versatile in garden designs and easy to care for. The trailing varieties are particularly good for pots, since they will flow over the edges, softening the design. Because hummingbirds and butterflies are fond of bright colors, choose a red variety for maximum impact in this garden. Sow the seeds indoors 6 to 8 weeks before planting outdoors or buy them in flats from your favorite garden center. In midsummer, cut the petunias back, especially if they've begun to look a bit straggly.

'CELEBRITY RED' PETUNIA

3. **FUCHSIA** *(Fuchsia* spp.)

CLASSIFICATION: Shrub

PLANT HARDINESS ZONES: Annual in all zones; perennial in 10 to 11

ULTIMATE SIZE: 12"–24" tall and 24"–36" wide

BLOOM TIME: Late spring to early autumn

SUN REQUIREMENT: Partial shade

Fuchsia's two-toned, pendant flowers are true showstoppers, and are hummingbird favorites, too. Fuchsias come in an array of colors: red, purple, pink, and white. Choose bright color combinations, such as red and purple or hot pink and purple, for your butterfly and hummingbird garden, and keep in mind that trailing varieties are best for containers and hanging baskets. Mist plants in hot weather, in addition to regular watering. Fuchsias will need to be moved to a frost-free location in winter, ideally to a sunroom or heated porch, since they are tender plants and will not overwinter outdoors except in zones 10 and 11.

'DAVID' FUCHSIA

'SALSA' SALVIA

4. SALVIA   (*Salvia* x *splendens*)

CLASSIFICATION: Annual
PLANT HARDINESS ZONES: All zones
ULTIMATE SIZE: 8"–15" tall and 8"–12" wide
BLOOM TIME: Summer
SUN REQUIREMENT: Full sun

Salvias, with their dense flower spikes, are attractive to butterflies and hummingbirds. There are dozens of cultivars, and all are both long-blooming and heat-tolerant, making them especially valuable plants for the summer container garden. Snip off passed flowers to promote further bloom and prune back in autumn to encourage new growth. In addition to the annual salvia shown here, there are many perennial salvias, which also draw butterflies and hummingbirds. Perennial salvias, more commonly called sages, are mainly available in the blue-purple color range and are hardy in zones 4 to 9.

5. ZINNIAS   (*Zinnia* spp.)

CLASSIFICATION: Annual
PLANT HARDINESS ZONES: All zones
ULTIMATE SIZE: 6"–25" tall and 6"–8" wide
BLOOM TIME: Midsummer through autumn
SUN REQUIREMENT: Full sun

With their fine range of warm colors and lovely full heads, zinnias are beloved garden plants. A color mix, like the 'Buttons' cultivar pictured here, is a good choice for the visual interest it offers in the container. Sow the seeds directly in the container after all danger of frost has passed, or start them indoors 4 weeks before you intend to plant outdoors. You can also purchase zinnias in flats. These flowers need good air circulation, so space them 12 inches apart. Water the plant at the soil level, keeping the leaves dry, to help prevent disease.

'BUTTONS' ZINNIA

6. ROSE MALLOW *(Hibiscus moscheutos)*

CLASSIFICATION: Perennial
PLANT HARDINESS ZONES: 5 to 11
ULTIMATE SIZE: 3'–5' tall and 1'–2' wide
BLOOM TIME: Summer til frost
SUN REQUIREMENT: Full sun to partial shade

This perennial is so tall and sturdy it is often mistaken for a shrub. The flowers, which are offered in red, pink, and white, are enormous, sometimes as large as 10 inches across. Choose a red variety for this design, as it will attract more butterflies and hummingbirds than the other shades. Rose mallow does best in a sunny spot that has some protection from the hot afternoon rays, and must be kept consistently moist.

ROSE MALLOW

'WALKER'S LOW' CATMINT

7. CATMINT *(Nepeta x faassenii)*

CLASSIFICATION: Perennial
PLANT HARDINESS ZONES: 4 to 9
ULTIMATE SIZE: 12" to 15" tall and wide
BLOOM TIME: Summer
SUN REQUIREMENT: Full sun

Free-flowering catmint produces spires of small, purple flowers above fragrant foliage of an attractive gray-green. After it has finished flowering, cut it back by about half to maintain its compact form (it may even flower again). Related to mint, this hardy plant is drought-tolerant and low-maintenance. Note that, in addition to butterflies, this plant attracts cats!

A CHILDREN'S VEGETABLE GARDEN

Sharing the gardening experience with young children can be a joyous adventure. And children cherish the sense of accomplishment and purpose they gain when they see the results of their efforts. They realize they can actually grow their own food, and have fun while they're doing it.

This potted garden contains easy-to-grow vegetables along with a few fun flowers. It is designed for ease of maintenance and maximum yield in a small space. Some of the plants—beans, peas, zucchini, lettuce, sunflowers, and zinnias—are easy to grow from seed. The tomatoes, eggplant, parsley, chives, and bell peppers are best purchased as small plants. Scallions grow from tiny "sets."

Plant this garden in full sun, close to a water source, after the danger of frost has passed. Note that there is no bloom time given for the vegetables in "Getting to Know the Plants"; though the plants do bloom briefly, they are generally not considered ornamental.

YOU WILL NEED...

- 10 pots of various sizes, if you are following the plan exactly

- Drainage material—crockery shards, gravel, or Styrofoam peanuts

- Potting soil

- A wire tomato cage (available at garden centers)

- Twist ties, twine, or string, to help beans, peas, and tomatoes grow up their supports

- Wooden stakes, to support bell peppers, eggplant, and sunflowers as needed

- A trowel

- 6 bamboo poles, to make 2 tripods

- Fertilizer

PLANT LIST

1. Pole beans

2. Cherry tomatoes

3. Peas

4. Zucchini

5. Lettuce mix

6. Dwarf sunflower (*Helianthus* spp.)

7. Eggplant

8. Zinnia (*Zinnia* spp.)

9. Nasturtium (*Nasturtium* spp.)

10. Bell pepper

11. Scallions

12. Chives

13. Parsley

PLANTING THE CHILDREN'S VEGETABLE GARDEN, STEP BY STEP

Step 1: Begin with the pole bean container; add drainage material—pottery shards, gravel, or Styrofoam peanuts—to the bottom of the pot and fill with potting soil up to about 2 or 3 inches below rim of container. Make a tripod or teepee shape with three of the bamboo poles, tying them at the top with the twine, and insert it firmly into the soil.

Step 2: Sow the pole bean seeds, following instructions on the packets, around the legs of the tripod. Water them

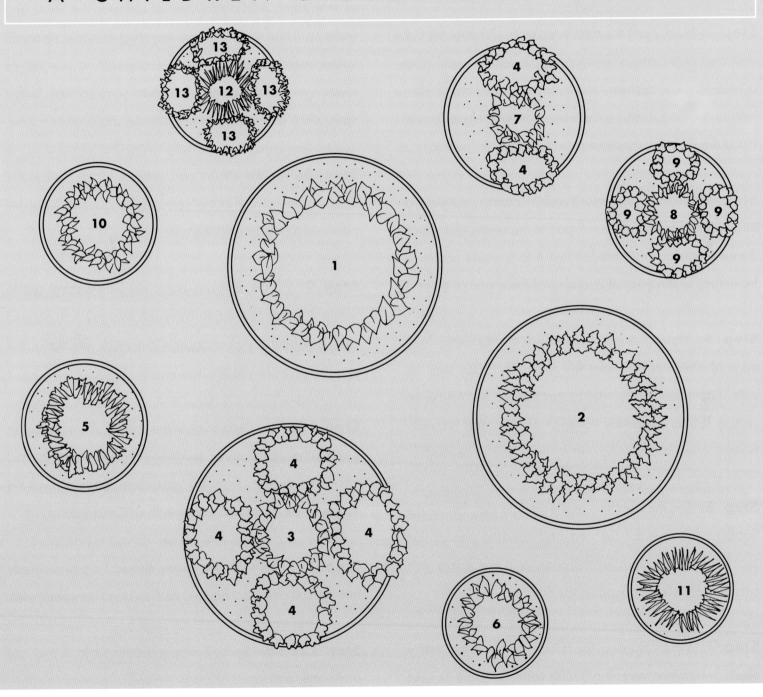

A CHILDREN'S VEGETABLE GARDEN

GETTING TO KNOW THE PLANTS

'BLUE LAKE SNAP' POLE BEAN

I. POLE BEANS

CLASSIFICATION: Annual
PLANT HARDINESS ZONES: All zones
ULTIMATE SIZE: 4'–5' tall and 6" wide
BLOOM TIME: None
SUN REQUIREMENT: Full sun

Pole beans are string beans that twine upwards. They are great because they keep bearing all summer long. 'Blue Lake Snap', shown here, is a good variety for fresh eating as well as for cooking, freezing, or canning. You can substitute a bush bean variety if you like, but you won't need the supporting tripod. The seeds can be sown directly in the soil after all danger of frost has passed.

2. CHERRY TOMATOES

CLASSIFICATION: Annual
PLANT HARDINESS ZONES: All zones
ULTIMATE SIZE: 3'–4' tall and
  2' wide
BLOOM TIME: None
SUN REQUIREMENT: Full sun

Great kid-pleasers, these plants produce clusters of tiny tomatoes perfect for snacking or salads. It's easiest to purchase tomato plants at a nursery; look for seedlings that are bushy and compact, avoiding any that appear stretched or yellow-green. There are dozens of good varieties. The tomatoes in this plan are grown in a wire cage, which makes tying them easier.

'SUN CHERRY' CHERRY TOMATO

PEAS

3. PEAS

CLASSIFICATION: Annual
PLANT HARDINESS ZONES: All zones
ULTIMATE SIZE: 3'–4' tall and 2' wide
BLOOM TIME: None
SUN REQUIREMENT: Full sun

Pea plants grow as vines, so they need a supporting tripod or teepee. Peas are a cool-season vegetable, and should be sown early in the spring (they will tolerate light frost). Sow them directly into the soil, and thin them to 4 inches apart once seedlings have come up. When days turn hot, the vines will most likely fade quickly. You can simply uproot them at that point (or put some zucchini in to replace them!). Try growing a snow pea variety for stir fry.

4. ZUCCHINI

CLASSIFICATION: Annual
PLANT HARDINESS ZONES: All zones
ULTIMATE SIZE: 1'–2' tall and to 5' wide
BLOOM TIME: Summer
SUN REQUIREMENT: Full sun

Zucchini is a bushy, easy-to-grow squash that is also easy to prepare. The seeds can be sown directly into the soil once all danger of frost has passed. Harvest the zucchini when they are still small and tender (no more than 6 inches long) or the plant will exhaust itself.

ZUCCHINI

5. LETTUCE MIX

CLASSIFICATION: Annual
PLANT HARDINESS ZONES: All zones
ULTIMATE SIZE: To 6" tall and wide
BLOOM TIME: None
SUN REQUIREMENT: Full sun

There are many different types of lettuce, including some that are colorful and ornamental enough for a flower garden. Leaf lettuce, which forms loose whorls of leaves rather than dense heads, is easiest to grow. Sow lettuce seeds directly into the soil and cover lightly with soil (light aids germination). Thin the seedlings to about 6 inches apart, though lettuce will accept some crowding. Lettuce is a cool season grower and will not thrive in very hot weather, though some varieties are more heat-tolerant than others.

LETTUCE MIX

'PACINO' DWARF SUNFLOWER

6. DWARF SUNFLOWER
(*Helianthus* spp.)

CLASSIFICATION: Annual
PLANT HARDINESS ZONES: All zones
ULTIMATE SIZE: To 3' tall, depending on
    variety
BLOOM TIME: Summer
SUN REQUIREMENT: Full sun

Prized for their tasty seeds, sunflowers produce beautiful yellow to russet-colored flower heads on thick, slightly prickly stems. Dozens of varieties are readily available. The dwarf varieties are particularly well suited for growing in pots, but even these may need staking, particularly if they are in a spot with some wind. Sow sunflowers seeds directly into the soil after all danger of frost has passed (they don't transplant well, so should not be started early indoors).

GOOD DWARF SUNFLOWERS
Here are some excellent, readily available dwarf sunflowers for pot culture:

'Music Box Mixed'—a colorful range of
    cream through yellow, including some
    two-toned deep red ones

'Teddy Bear'—bright yellow, very fluffy
    double blooms

'Sunspot Dwarf'—giant yellow blooms up
    to 10 inches wide

'Incredible'—bears big blooms but grows
    just 15 inches tall

'Big Smile'—cheery yellow blooms with a
    chocolate brown eye

'Pacino'—lovely yellow flowers, heavy
    blooming

7. EGGPLANT

CLASSIFICATION: Annual
PLANT HARDINESS ZONES: All zones
ULTIMATE SIZE: To 1'–2' tall and wide
BLOOM TIME: None
SUN REQUIREMENT: Full sun

One of the most beautiful of vegetables, eggplant may not be your child's favorite now, but after he or she has nurtured its growth, attitudes may change! Try any of the varieties on the market, including whites, pale purples, and miniatures. Purchase these plants as seedlings from your garden center.

'NEON' EGGPLANT

'SCARLET SPLENDOR' ZINNIA

8. ZINNIA (*Zinnia* spp.)

CLASSIFICATION: Annual
PLANT HARDINESS ZONES: All zones
ULTIMATE SIZE: 6"–25" tall and 6"–8" wide
BLOOM TIME: Midsummer through autumn
SUN REQUIREMENT: Full sun

Among the easiest of all annuals to grow, zinnias have been broadly hybridized to produce many forms and colors. Let your child browse through the racks of seed packets, or the pages of seed catalogs, to select his or her favorites. Sow the seeds directly in the container after all danger of frost, or start them indoors 4 weeks before you intend to plant outdoors (you can also purchase zinnias in flats). These flowers need good air circulation, so make sure to space them 12 inches apart. Water the plant at the soil level, keeping the leaves dry, to help prevent disease.

9. NASTURTIUM (*Tropaeolum majus*)

CLASSIFICATION: Annual
PLANT HARDINESS ZONES: All zones
ULTIMATE SIZE: 1'–8' tall, depending on type, and 2' wide
BLOOM TIME: Summer
SUN REQUIREMENT: Full sun to partial shade

The climbing varieties can reach 8' tall or more, while some others will remain fairly compact—read the description of the type you are buying. If you plant the climbing kind without a support (as in this plan), it will happily trail out of the pot and along the ground. The cheerful red, orange, or yellow flowers are edible, as are the leaves, and add a wonderful peppery flavor to garden salads. Sow the seeds directly in the soil after frost danger.

'EMPRESS OF INDIA' NASTURTIUM

10. BELL PEPPER

CLASSIFICATION: Annual
PLANT HARDINESS ZONES: All zones
ULTIMATE SIZE: 1'–3' tall and 1'–2' wide
BLOOM TIME: None
SUN REQUIREMENT: Full sun

Most bell peppers may be harvested while green, or left on the plant to ripen to a sweeter red. When purchasing, look for with healthy, compact seedlings (you could also start your seeds indoors, 6 to 8 weeks before you intend to plant your garden outdoors). Select from many varieties of sweet peppers, and add some hot peppers too.

'BLUSHING BEAUTY' BELL PEPPER

SCALLION

11. SCALLIONS

CLASSIFICATION: Annual
PLANT HARDINESS ZONES: All zones
ULTIMATE SIZE: To 2' tall and 4" wide
BLOOM TIME: None
SUN REQUIREMENT: Full sun

Also called green onions, scallions are great in salads and stir fry. Select "sets," which are immature bulbs, in early spring, or plant long-day variety seeds in spring. If you plan to use them, pull them up while they are still tender.

CHIVES

12. CHIVES

CLASSIFICATION: Perennial
PLANT HARDINESS ZONES: 3 to 9
ULTIMATE SIZE: 12"–18" tall and
  6"–8" wide
BLOOM TIME: Summer
SUN REQUIREMENT: Full sun

Related to onions, chives can be snipped with scissors and used as a flavoring for salads or meat dishes or sprinkled atop sour cream–slathered baked potatoes. The plant also produces globe-shaped, crisply textured pink flower heads, which are highly decorative (and edible, too). These plants can be overwintered indoors, after they've been let to die down through a frost or two (they require a short dormant period).

PARSLEY

13. PARSLEY

CLASSIFICATION: Biennial, grown as an annual
PLANT HARDINESS ZONES: All zones as annual
ULTIMATE SIZE: 6"–2' tall and 1'–3' wide
BLOOM TIME: None
SUN REQUIREMENT: Full sun

Curly parsley makes a great garnish, can be used for seasoning, and is rich in Vitamin C. It is also very pretty as a companion plant in potted gardens. Usually grown as an annual, it will overwinter in mild climates (but is never as good the second year). It's slow to start from seed, so begin with small nursery-grown plants.

A HALF-BARREL WATER GARDEN

Water features, from ponds and streams to fountains and formal pools, have graced gardens for centuries, lending a serene aura to the space. But gardeners with little time and no room for a full-sized garden pool can also enjoy the soothing effects of a water planting. The water garden featured here is contained in one large waterproof container; use either a plastic tub set into a wooden half-barrel or a container intended for a water garden (check garden centers and mail-order suppliers). This garden is relatively simple to install and to maintain, yet has enough plant variety to provide interesting texture, shape, and color.

Except in frost-free areas, plants for small water gardens should be treated as annuals. In warm climates, the water garden can be kept going year-round. It's possible to overwinter a water lily, but it requires more of a commitment than most gardeners wish to invest. If you'd like to try overwintering, see the Calendar of Care on page 69.

Site this garden on a sunny, level spot, preferably next to a garden wall or fence where the garden will get a bit of shade in the afternoon. It's also best to place your half-barrel within reach of a hose. You'll have to top the water level off from time to time, and hauling heavy buckets of water can be a chore. Water gardens in general require a bit more maintenance than most other potted gardens, but be assured that the rewards are well worth the extra effort.

PLANTING THE HALF-BARREL WATER GARDEN, STEP BY STEP

Step 1: First, make sure you have the container positioned where you want it; once you've filled it with water, you won't be able to move it. Fill the container with water to a little more than half and let it sit for several days, allowing the temperature to regulate and the chemicals in the water to dissipate.

Step 2: In most small water gardens, the plants are best contained in pots, then submerged in the garden container. Use heavy topsoil or rich garden loam in the pots (regular potting soil is too light, and will float to the surface in a scummy mess).

Step 3: To plant the water lily, fill the pot one-third full of heavy soil and add a fertilizer tablet. Fill the pot the rest of the way with soil and drench it to get rid of air pockets. Insert the water lily tuber or rhizome into the soil, making sure the growing point is free of soil. Water once more, then gently add small stones or gravel to the top, to prevent the soil from washing away.

YOU WILL NEED...

- A waterproof container 2 to 3 feet wide and deep (it can be smaller if you decide not to plant the water lily)

- A hose that reaches to your garden site

- 5 terra-cotta or plastic pots (1 gallon or larger for the water lily)

- Several bricks or terra-cotta pots, to raise the height of the submerged pots

- Soil—don't use regular container potting soil; instead, ask for rich topsoil or garden loam, which are heavier

- Small stones or gravel

- A fish or two, if desired

- Fertilizer tablets, available from water garden suppliers

PLANT LIST

1. Water lily (*Nymphaea* spp.)
2. Parrot's feather (*Myriophyllum aquaticum*)
3. Water hyacinth (*Eichhornia crassipes*)
4. Dwarf cattail (*Typha* 'Minima')
5. Water lily (*Nymphaea* spp.)

A HALF-BARREL WATER GARDEN

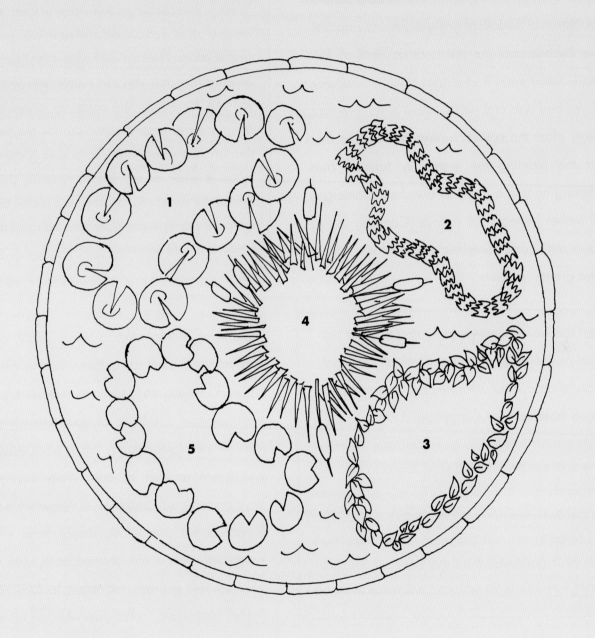

GETTING TO KNOW THE PLANTS

'ATTRACTION' WATER LILY

1 & 5. WATER LILY   (*Nymphaea* spp.)

CLASSIFICATION: Aquatic
PLANT HARDINESS ZONES: Depends on water lily type
ULTIMATE SIZE: Depends on type
BLOOM TIME: Summer
SUN REQUIREMENT: Full sun to part shade

While this plan suggests two water lilies, the size of your water garden will dictate whether you can accommodate both. These plants tend to need a fair amount of room, so ask for a compact water lily variety when ordering. You may also pot the two lilies together in one very large pot. Some water lilies are hardy, and may overwinter in zones 4 or 5 and above (they can survive in their pot as long as the roots aren't allowed to freeze). Others are tropical, and will survive outdoors only in zones 9 and 10. Most beginning water gardeners treat water lilies as annuals, throwing them out and simply reinvesting in new ones the following year.

'MARLIAC WHITE' WATER LILY

WATER LILY SUBSTITUTE

If you are considering a small container that won't harbor a water lily comfortably, consider substituting water snowflake (*Nymphoides* spp.). This is a fast-growing plant with heart-shaped leaves and small white or yellow flowers that look a bit like small water lilies.

PARROT'S FEATHER

2. PARROT'S FEATHER (*Myriophyllum aquaticum*)

CLASSIFICATION: Oxygenating aquatic plant
PLANT HARDINESS ZONES: Not applicable
ULTIMATE SIZE: 2" to 4" tall and spreading
BLOOM TIME: None
SUN REQUIREMENT: Full sun to partial shade

The brilliant green stems lined with feathery leaves give this plant its fanciful name. It will contribute oxygen to your garden, helping to sustain the fish, and will help crowd out algae. Grow it in a pot sunk beneath the water's surface. Though relatively hardy, parrot's feather is inexpensive enough to be grown as an annual, since it's hardly worth the bother to overwinter it.

WATER HYACINTH

3. WATER HYACINTH (*Eichhornia crassipes*)

CLASSIFICATION: Floating perennial
  aquatic
PLANT HARDINESS ZONES: 9 to 11
ULTIMATE SIZE: 6" tall and spreading
BLOOM TIME: Summer
SUN REQUIREMENT: Full sun

This is a pretty plant that is a major pest in the waterways of the South. Planted safely in your container, it can do no harm. It has shiny green leaves and showy purple flowers. Like other tender water plants, treat it as an annual.

Dwarf Cattail

4. DWARF CATTAIL   (*Typha* 'Minima')

CLASSIFICATION: Marginal aquatic
PLANT HARDINESS ZONES: 3 to 10
ULTIMATE SIZE: To 2' tall and 1' wide
BLOOM TIME: Late summer
SUN REQUIREMENT: Full sun to partial shade

This classic water plant provides handsome vertical accent to your container garden—the variety 'Minima' is an excellent dwarf selection. The brown catkins are actually the flowers, and these appear late in the summer. Cattails should be planted no deeper than 12 inches beneath the water's surface, so set the container on an upended pot (as described in "Planting the Half-Barrel Water Garden") if your container is deeper than that.

A GARDEN OF KITCHEN HERBS

Herbs are among the easiest plants to grow, demanding little expense or effort. And the reward—fresh herbs to flavor light summer fare, with plenty left over to dry for seasoning winter dishes—far outweighs the minimal work these tough plants require.

The herb garden outlined here includes a combination of perennial, half-hardy, and annual plants. Given a little care, the perennial herbs (sage, chives, thyme, oregano, and chamomile) will prosper for several years, but may eventually become too large for the space. They can be transplanted to their own pots or to an appropriate spot in the garden. Rosemary can survive winters in warmer climates (in areas where winter temperatures never drop below 0 degrees Fahrenheit) or can be removed from the container and grown as a houseplant where winters are colder. The annual herbs (dill, basil, parsley, and nasturtiums) will not survive a hard frost, and should be discarded at the end of the season.

Plant this garden in spring, after all danger of frost has passed, and site it in a sunny spot. Most herbs are native to the Mediterranean, and in addition to full sun, they like a sandier soil than most other potted plants. You'll only need one of each plant in this plan (but note that there are two places for thyme, basil, and parsley on the plan, so that you can choose two different varieties of each). Most herbs are best purchased as seedlings, but you can also start some of the annuals from seed, 6 to 12 weeks before you intend to plant outdoors (follow the specific directions on the seed packet).

YOU WILL NEED...

- 1 large container—a half-barrel is ideal (must have holes for drainage); alternatively, use an oversized terra-cotta pot or a collection of smaller pots

- Drainage material, such as broken crockery, gravel, or Styrofoam peanuts

- Sandy potting soil (mix 3 parts commercial potting soil and 1 part coarse sand)

- A trowel

- Garden snips or scissors for harvesting

- Fertilizer

- Garden markers, for identifying plants (optional)

PLANT LIST

1. Rosemary (*Rosmarinus officinalis*)
2. Dill (*Anthemum graveolens*)
3. Chamomile (*Chamaemelum nobile*)
4. Parsley (*Petrolinum crispum*)
5. Thyme (*Thymus vulgaris*)
6. Nasturtium (*Tropaeolum majus*)
7. Chives (*Allium schoenoprasum*)
8. Basil (*Ocimum basilicum*)
9. Sage (*Salvia officinalis*)
10. Greek or Golden oregano (*Origanum vulgare* ssp. *hirtum*)

PLANTING THE GARDEN OF KITCHEN HERBS, STEP BY STEP

Step 1: Prepare the container by first adding drainage material—because herbs like sharp drainage, make sure there are about two inches of coarse gravel or Styrofoam peanuts on the bottom of the container. Then fill the container with the sandy potting mix to within 3 inches of the top. Water thoroughly and allow soil to settle. Add enough soil for it to sit within 3 inches of top of container.

Step 2: Remove one herb at a time from its pot. Use care, as root systems may not be fully developed in young plants.

A GARDEN OF KITCHEN HERBS

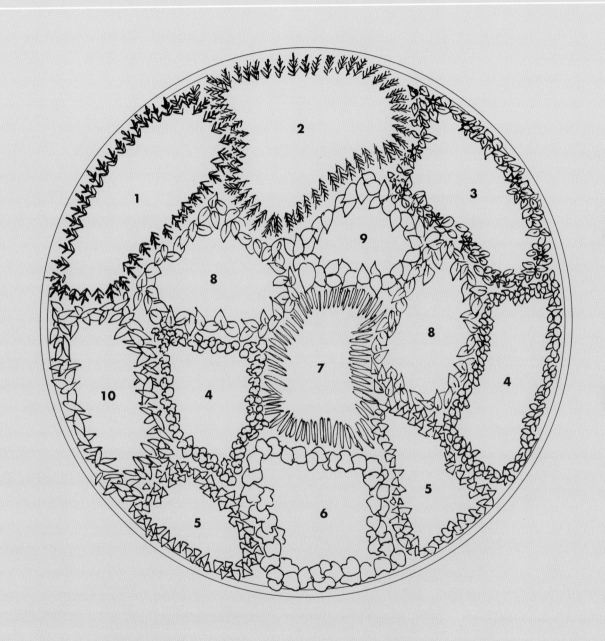

Step 3: If the container is positioned in a corner and will be seen from the front, install the plants as indicated on the plan, digging small holes for each, then firming the soil around the plant's base. Begin with the dill, chamomile, and rosemary at the back of the container and work forward, finishing with the herbs on the outside front and side edges. If the container will be seen from all sides, place tall plants (dill and chamomile) at center; then install the basil, rosemary, and sage in a ring around the dill and chamomile; and the remaining plants around the outside. Water well once you've finished installing all the plants.

SUBSTITUTE HERBS FOR THIS GARDEN

If your favorite herb is missing from the garden plan, cheer up: there are a number of herbs that can be substituted effectively in the plan. Just leave out one of the others on the diagram, and include one or more of the following instead. Or, plant a selection of these in pots to complement your main herb garden.

* Coriander/cilantro (*Coriandrum sativum*)—Substitute this annual for one of the basil or thyme plants; it's especially useful in Mexican and Chinese cooking.

* Lemongrass (*Cymbopogon citratus*)—Substitute this tender perennial (zones 8 to 10) for the chamomile or a basil, if you favor Thai and other Asian cuisines.

* Fennel (*Foeniculum vulgare*)—Substitute this hardy perennial (to Zone 4) for the dill; it has an unusual anise or licorice flavor.

* Summer savory (*Satureja hortensis*)—This annual adds a peppery flavor to salads, cheeses, vegetables, and meat dishes. Substitute it for one of the basils.

* Marjoram (*Origanum majorana*)—Substitute this tender perennnial (to Zone 7) for one of the thymes. It adds a delicate flavor to fish and poultry dishes.

* Mint (*Mentha* spp.)—This hardy perennial (to Zone 3) is perfect for flavoring iced tea and making mint sauce. Because this is an aggressive, invasive plant, don't use it in the main container garden; instead, grow it in a separate pot.

CALENDAR OF CARE

SPRING: *If you are starting seeds of annual herbs indoors, sow them 6 to 12 weeks before the last frost date, following suggestions on seed packets. Check the condition of perennial herbs, trimming dead or damaged wood and removing plants that have outgrown the container or are no longer healthy enough to keep. Add or replace perennial herbs as soon as soil is workable. Plant annual and tender perennial herbs after the last frost.*

SUMMER: *Water the container regularly. Harvest the herbs regularly, as cutting will promote tender new growth. Herbs typically fare well in poor soils, so fertilize only once or twice during the summer.*

AUTUMN: *Harvest the last of annual herbs before the first frost (they can be dried or frozen for winter use). Remove tender perennial herbs in cold climates and grow indoors. Hardy herbs may survive outdoors over the winter (or you can remove them indoors with the others). If you decide to try them outdoors, make sure that*

the container is situated against a sheltering wall; nestle bags filled with dry leaves around the container.

WINTER: *Remove any vulnerable pots to a frost-free location before freezing weather arrives.*

PINCHING BACK HERBS

To grow thicker, bushier herbs, pinch off flower buds of basil, sage, and parsley as they appear. You can allow the chives to bloom; once the chive flowers have faded, cut the plant back to about 3 inches and it will send out new growth for future harvesting. Thyme, rosemary, chamomile, and oregano plants will bloom without much effect on the plants' culinary use. Nasturtiums are grown for their flowers as well as the leaves—use the showy orange, yellow, or red blooms, which have a peppery flavor similar to watercress, in salads or even tea sandwiches.

GETTING TO KNOW THE PLANTS

'ARP' ROSEMARY

1. ROSEMARY
(Rosmarinus officinalis)

CLASSIFICATION: Tender perennial; grown as
  annual outside its hardiness zones
PLANT HARDINESS ZONES: 8 to 10
ULTIMATE SIZE: 2'–3' tall and as wide
BLOOM TIME: Summer
SUN REQUIREMENT: Full sun

An elegant herb with thin, somewhat leathery
and often fuzzy leaves, rosemary is used in classic French cooking, lending a distinct flavor to
roast chicken and pork. It is often combined
with grilled vegetables and is almost always
included in a bouquet garni. It is fairly drought-
tolerant, and tolerates heat well. Rosemary
plants will last for many years, becoming woody
over time. In cool climates, protect it with a
layer of mulch or repot it and bring it indoors
for the winter.

2. DILL (*Anthemum graveolens*)

CLASSIFICATION: Annual
PLANT HARDINESS ZONES: All zones
ULTIMATE SIZE: To 3' tall and 2' wide
BLOOM TIME: Summer
SUN REQUIREMENT: Full sun

The perfect accompaniment to fish dishes, dill is also a key ingredient in dill pickles. The seeds have culinary uses as well. Allow a few flowers to develop at the end of the growing season in order to collect the seeds. Dill foliage is bright green and finely feathered, and it bears pretty yellow umbels of flowers. If you want a more compact plant, try a dwarf variety such as 'Fern Leaf' or 'Dukat'.

DILL

CHAMOMILE

3. CHAMOMILE
(*Chamaemelum nobile*)

CLASSIFICATION: Perennial
PLANT HARDINESS ZONES: 3 to 9
ULTIMATE SIZE: 3"–10" tall and
    12" wide
BLOOM TIME: Summer
SUN REQUIREMENT: Full sun

Prized for their soothing qualities when dried, chamomile's leaves are often brewed as a tea. Chamomile is also one of the prettiest herbs in this garden; it has delicate, feathery leaves and tiny daisy-like flowers. Like most herbs, it prefers light, sandy soil and lots of sun. It is fairly hardy, and will survive most winters.

ITALIAN BROADLEAF PARSLEY AND CURLY PARSLEY

4. PARSLEY (*Petrolinum crispum*)

CLASSIFICATION: Biennial (grown as annual)
PLANT HARDINESS ZONES: All zones
ULTIMATE SIZE: 1'–2' tall and wide
BLOOM TIME: None
SUN REQUIREMENT: Full sun

Probably the best-known herb, parsley is also one of the easiest to grow. Used for flavor and as a garnish, curly parsley has dense, almost frilly clumps of bright green foliage. Italian parsley (*Petrolinum crispum* var. *neapolitanum*) adds a fresh, strong flavor to sauces and stews. While parsley is technically a biennial, and so will come back the second year, it never performs as well as it did the first year. Most gardeners prefer to pull it up after the growing season and start over the next year.

5. THYME (*Thymus vulgaris*)

CLASSIFICATION: Perennial
PLANT HARDINESS ZONES: 5 to 9
ULTIMATE SIZE: 6"–12" tall and wide
BLOOM TIME: Summer
SUN REQUIREMENT: Full sun

Species thyme (*Thymus vulgaris*) is remarkably easy to grow, and is an excellent culinary herb, valued for its contributions to meats, poultry, vegetables, soups, and stews. But there are many other types of thyme available, and you may wish to experiment with these for variety: try caraway thyme (*Thymus herba-barona*) or lemon thyme (*T.* x *citriodorus*).

Thyme has few requirements, but does like well-drained soil. After a few years, this perennial may look woody and unkempt; at this point it's best to simply dig it up and replace it.

THYME

NASTURTIUM

6. NASTURTIUM *(Tropaeolum majus)*

CLASSIFICATION: Annual
PLANT HARDINESS ZONES: All zones
ULTIMATE SIZE: 1'–8' tall, depending on type, and 2' wide
BLOOM TIME: Summer
SUN REQUIREMENT: Full sun

Frequently grown simply for their showy red, yellow, or orange flowers, nasturtiums are vinelike and sprawling. The climbing varieties can reach 8 feet tall or more, while some others will remain fairly compact—read the description of the type you are buying. If you plant it without a support (as in this plan), it will happily trail out of the pot and along the ground. Both the bright green, heavily-veined, round leaves and the vivid flowers are edible and have a peppery flavor. Sow the seeds directly in the soil after frost danger has passed.

CHIVES

7. CHIVES (*Allium schoenoprasum*)

CLASSIFICATION: Perennial
PLANT HARDINESS ZONES: 3 to 9
ULTIMATE SIZE: 12"–18" tall and 6"–8" wide
BLOOM TIME: Summer
SUN REQUIREMENT: Full sun

Related to onions and garlic, chives have a milder flavor than their cousins. A versatile culinary herb, chives are harvested by snipping the dark green, hollow stems, which are also easy to dry. The plant produces globe-shaped, pink flower heads, which are highly decorative (and edible, too). These plants can be overwintered indoors, so you can continue to use them, after they've been let to die down through a frost or two (they require a short dormant period). Or simply protect the container as described in "Winter Care" on page 16, and watch them come back next year.

8. BASIL (*Ocimum basilicum*)

CLASSIFICATION: Annual
PLANT HARDINESS ZONES: All zones
ULTIMATE SIZE: 2' tall and 1' wide
BLOOM TIME: None
SUN REQUIREMENT: Full sun

The perfect companion to sliced fresh tomatoes and the essential ingredient for pesto, basil is a favorite of many herb gardeners. Among the easiest herbs to grow, its only demands are good drainage and plenty of water. Purple basil, while very pretty, is not as flavorful. Harvesting the leaves regularly helps the plant stay compact. Small, insignificant flowers appear in late summer; pinch these off to ensure a continued harvest of leaves.

BASIL

GOOD BASILS

Lemon basil (*O. basilicum citriodorum*)—lemony scent and flavor • Bush basil (*O. minimum*)—a compact basil especially good for pots • 'Cinnamon' basil—cinnamon flavor and fragrance • 'Purple Ruffles' basil—decorative, ruffled, purple leaves • 'Spicy Globe' basil—small, flavorful leaves

9. SAGE (*Salvia officinalis*)

CLASSIFICATION: Perennial
PLANT HARDINESS ZONES: 4 to 8
ULTIMATE SIZE: 1'–3' tall and wide
BLOOM TIME: Summer
SUN REQUIREMENT: Full sun

Sage has distinctive elongated gray-green, sandpapery leaves on woody stems. The leaves of this highly aromatic plant are commonly used to flavor poultry, fish, and sausages; sometimes they are coated with batter and deep fried for a Mediterranean-style treat. The leaves also dry well for later use. Protect sage for the winter and prune it back hard in the spring, to keep it in bounds. Over time, it will become woody, so you will most likely neex to replace this plant after a few years.

SAGE

GREEK OREGANO

10. GREEK OR GOLDEN OREGANO

(*Origanum vulgare* ssp. *hirtum*)

CLASSIFICATION: Perennial
PLANT HARDINESS ZONES: 4 to 9
ULTIMATE SIZE: To 2' tall and wide
BLOOM TIME: Summer
SUN REQUIREMENT: Full sun

An essential ingredient for Italian cuisine, oregano is most often used to flavor tomato sauces. It is a low-growing plant with tiny dark green or golden leaves and in late summer, delicate white or pink flowers. Another heat-lover, oregano produces excess oil in very warm weather, leading to more fragrant, flavorful leaves. Greek or golden oregano is the most flavorful, but if you are having trouble finding it, plant the straight species (*O. vulgare*) or one of its worthy cultivars.

A FRAGRANT GARDEN

While color may be the first thing gardening enthusiasts consider when selecting plants, fragrance is probably a close second. There are few things more evocative than scent—the perfume of roses calls to mind summer afternoons in Grandmother's garden; the spicy aroma of carnations brings back romantic memories of prom corsages; and the heavenly scent of lilies of the valley recall exuberant spring weddings.

While few gardens are devoted solely to scent, it is possible to create an attractive garden in which fragrant plants take center stage. This potted garden features a long-blooming, relatively easy-care rose, lush lavender, and other sweetly scented partners. All these plants are designed to work well together on a deck, patio, or balcony, though you will need to adjust the number and arrangement of pots depending on your situation. We've shown them clustered around the steps of a patio, but the plan can be easily adapted—just make sure to site the garden in full sun (and note that we've purposefully located the rose—with its fierce thorns—out of the traffic flow).

PLANTING THE FRAGRANT GARDEN, STEP BY STEP

Step 1: Begin with the rose planter, layering the drainage material on the bottom of the pot and filling the container to about half full with potting mix. Carefully, while wearing gardening gloves, remove the rose from its pot, taking care not to break any branches. If the rose container arrived with special food, mix the granules with the soil in your pot. Examine the roots; if they are growing upward or in a circular fashion, gently loosen the roots from the soil. Place the plant in the prepared pot, and fill in with more potting soil, pressing it down with a trowel or your hand. Water thoroughly until water flows through drainage holes. Allow soil to settle and add more as needed to fill pot to within 2 or 3 inches of the rim.

Step 2: Plant the two lavender pots using the same method employed for the rose (above). If you are using sizable pots, make sure to position them in their permanent place before filling, as they will be very heavy once potting soil and plants are in place.

Step 3: Next, plant the pots containing the cottage pinks and the white alyssum. Prepare the container with drainage

YOU WILL NEED...

* 7 containers of various sizes (if planting the garden exactly as shown), plus 2 more for the lilies; the rose will require a minimum depth and width of 18"

* Drainage material—broken terra-cotta pot pieces, gravel, or Styrofoam peanuts

* Potting soil (add 1 part coarse sand 2 parts potting soil for the pot containing lavender)

* A trowel

* Fertilizer

* Pruning shears

PLANT LIST

1. 'Flower Carpet White' rose (*Rosa* x 'Flower Carpet White')

2. Lavender (*Lavandula angustifolia*)

3. Cottage pink (*Dianthus plumarius*)

4. White alyssum (*Lobularia maritima*)

5. Flowering tobacco (*Nicotiana alata*)

6. Heliotrope (*Heliotropium arborescens*)

7. Scented geranium (*Pelargonium* spp.)

8. Purple alyssum (*Lobularia maritima*)

9. Star gazer lily (*Lilium* 'Star Gazer')

A FRAGRANT GARDEN

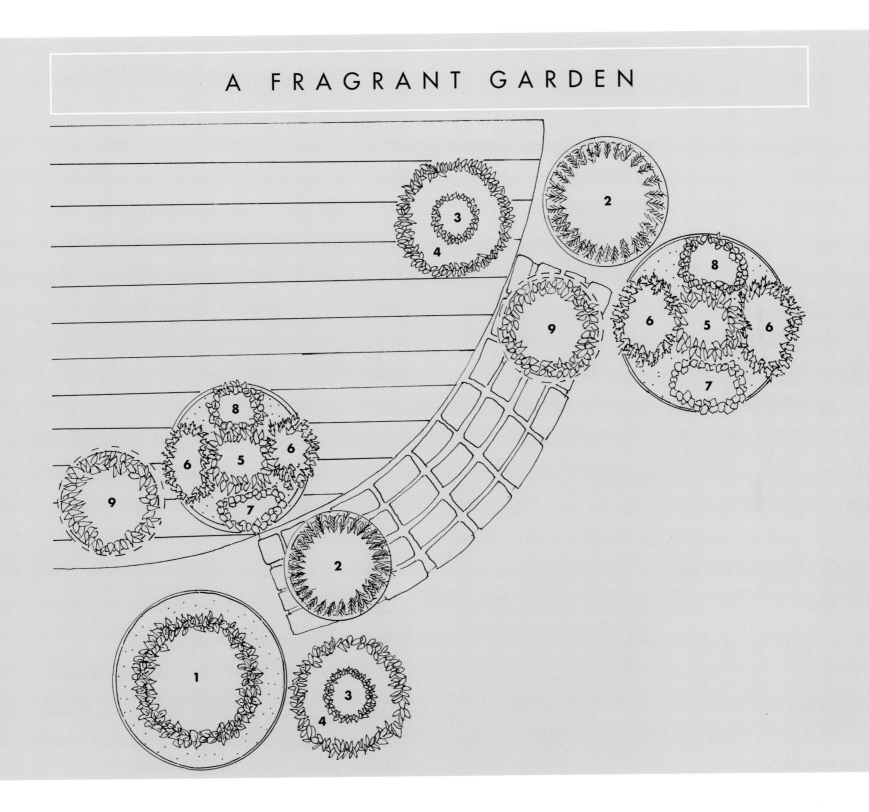

material and fill about three-quarters full with potting mix. Remove the cottage pinks from their containers, loosen their roots, and place them at the center of the pot, pressing gently into the soil. Remove alyssum plants (about 3 per pot should do it) from their containers, loosen their roots, and place them in a circle around the cottage pinks allowing them to drape over the side of the pot. (They will probably be too small to do much draping as yet, but give them a bit of time and they will fill in admirably.) Fill the pot with more soil, carefully pressing it down between the plants and between the roots and the sides of the container, and water well. Add more soil as needed.

Step 4: Next, plant the containers that feature the heliotrope, nicotiana, scented geranium, and purple alyssum. Prepare the containers with drainage material and fill to about three-quarters with potting mix. Remove heliotrope and flowering tobacco from their containers, loosen roots, and place according to the plan (adjust to your preference), pressing them lightly into soil. Remove scented geraniums from their containers, loosen roots, and place on either side of, but slightly in front of the heliotrope, so that they drape over the sides of the planter. Press lightly into soil. Remove purple alyssum from the containers, loosen roots, and place one between the other plants and around the edges of the container, allowing them to drape over

the sides. Fill the pot with more soil, carefully pressing it down between the plants and between the roots and the sides of the container. Water well and add more soil as needed.

Step 5: If possible, the lily is best brought out when it is flowering, but left in an inconspicuous place before and after it flowers, when its stalks are less than gorgeous. Plant the lily bulbs (you can plant 3 to a pot) in spring, 8 inches deep in the potting soil. Fertilize the bulbs in autumn. As frost approaches, protect the pots by positioning them against a sheltering wall and nestling bags of dry leaves among them.

PRUNING THE ROSE

In early spring, before the plant gets leaves, prune the branches back by about one-third, using sharp, clean pruners. Make the cut just above a bud (there will be a tiny node) at a sharp angle away from the center of the plant. Be sure to wear gloves when you prune, as the 'Flower Carpet White' rose has especially fierce thorns.

CALENDAR OF CARE

SPRING: *Plant this garden initially in spring, after all danger of frost has passed. Prune roses, as described on the opposite page. The spring after initial planting, check the rose and lavender for new leaves, to ensure that they have survived the winter. If they have not, purchase replacements. Purchase annuals and tender perennials in spring for planting after the last frost date. The cottage pinks, flowering tobacco, and alyssum may be started from seed indoors, about 6 to 8 weeks before the last predicted frost.*

Also in spring, return lavender plants to pots and cut away any dead twigs.

SUMMER: *Water your containers daily in hot, dry weather. Fertilize mixed planters with water-soluble mixture (using formula suggested on package) as follows: one week after planting; one-third of the way through the summer season; and again two-thirds of the way through the season. For maximum bloom, purchase special rose food and fertilize as the package instructs. Deadhead the roses, heliotrope, flowering tobacco, and alyssum as needed. If lavender becomes leggy, cut it back by about one-third to allow for fresh new growth. Cut back after flowers have faded.*

AUTUMN: *In temperate and cold climates, remove scented geraniums from planters before first frost and overwinter them indoors or in a greenhouse. Remove and discard annuals after a killing frost or when they appear to be spent.*

WINTER: *In cold climates (zones 7 and north), wrap the carpet rose, any large pots of lavender, and the lily pots in burlap or bubble wrap. Place them against a sheltering wall and nestle bags of dry leaves among them.*

GETTING TO KNOW THE PLANTS

'FLOWER CARPET WHITE' ROSE

1. 'FLOWER CARPET WHITE' ROSE
(*Rosa* x 'Flower Carpet White')

CLASSIFICATION: Groundcover rose
PLANT HARDINESS ZONES: 3 to 10
ULTIMATE SIZE: 3' tall and wide
BLOOM TIME: Late spring to autumn
SUN REQUIREMENT: Full sun

The Flower Carpet roses are among the easiest of all roses to care for, and they are resistant to most of the pests and diseases that plague less vigorous varieties. They reward even the most minimal care with an exceptionally long bloom period—from late spring to autumn in temperate climates. There are several different types of Flower Carpet; we've chosen white for this plan, but 'Flower Carpet Pink' would work just as well.

2. **LAVENDER** (*Lavandula angustifolia*)

CLASSIFICATION: Perennial
PLANT HARDINESS ZONES: 5 to 9
ULTIMATE SIZE: 2' to 3' tall and wide
BLOOM TIME: Summer
SUN REQUIREMENT: Full sun

A relative of mint, lavender is particularly popular in Europe, where it is grown as a field crop, especially in the south of France. Though it is evergreen in warmer climates, this woody aromatic plant prefers a somewhat sandy soil and does best with limited fertilizing. Lavender plants produce silvery green foliage and spikes of small purple blooms in summer. Good varieties include 'Munstead' and 'Hidcote'.

'MUNSTEAD' LAVENDER

DRYING LAVENDER

The fresh scent of lavender is nearly universally appealing, and it's possible, even easy, to preserve that fragrance for year-round enjoyment.

❋ First, grow at least 2 or 3 lavender plants, to provide an ample supply.

❋ Harvest some bloom stalks before flowers open. Cut the flower stems on a cool morning after the dew has dried with sharp flower snips, cutting the stems at their base.

❋ Gather the stems in small bundles, wrap with string or elastic bands, and hang upside down in a cool, dry, dark place until fully dry.

❋ Use in dried floral arrangements or as bouquets. Or remove the flower buds and add to potpourri; lavender buds are also wonderful in sachets.

❋ Save the trimmings from lavender plants to throw on the fire in winter. Though the scent is brief, it is heavenly.

'CYCLOPS' COTTAGE PINK

3. COTTAGE PINK *(Dianthus plumarius)*

CLASSIFICATION: Perennial
PLANT HARDINESS ZONES: 4 to 10
ULTIMATE SIZE: 6"–12" tall and 6"–8" wide
BLOOM TIME: Summer
SUN REQUIREMENT: Full sun

These spicy-sweet-fragranced relatives of carnations are among the easiest of plants to grow, and will reward even benign neglect with all-summer bloom in shades of pink, red, and white. The fringed petals of these old-fashioned favorites look like they've been snipped with pinking shears, hence their common name. Many gardeners grow these as annuals, as they are fairly short-lived, so try protecting them for the winter but be prepared to fill in with new plants if necessary.

4. WHITE ALYSSUM
(Lobularia maritima)

CLASSIFICATION: Annual
PLANT HARDINESS ZONES: All zones
ULTIMATE SIZE: 2"–8" tall and to 12" wide
BLOOM TIME: Late spring to autumn
SUN REQUIREMENT: Full sun to partial shade

This classic, easy-care filler plant produces mounds of blossoms held in tiny spheres, and in addition to the white of the species, now comes in shades of pink and purple. Sow seeds directly into the soil after frost danger, or plant seeds indoors 6 to 8 weeks before transplanting outdoors. You can also purchase alyssum in flats. Deadhead to promote further flowering.

WHITE ALYSSUM

5. FLOWERING TOBACCO (*Nicotiana alata*)

CLASSIFICATION: Annual
PLANT HARDINESS ZONES: All zones
ULTIMATE SIZE: 12"–15" tall
BLOOM TIME: Early summer til frost
SUN REQUIREMENT: Full sun to partial shade

Flowering tobacco is beautifully fragranced and bears star-shaped blooms available in a variety of colors, from red to pink to white to lime green. The scent is strongest late in the day, when the flowers open—a bonus for those who arrive home in the evening. Heat- and cold-tolerant, this popular flower is incredibly easygoing. Start seeds 4 to 6 weeks before you plan to plant them outdoors; light aids in germination of the seeds, so barely cover them with soil.

'THE PERFECT MIX' FLOWERING TOBACCO

'LEMOINE' HELIOTROPE

6. HELIOTROPE (*Heliotropium arborescens*)

CLASSIFICATION: Annual (perennial in warm climates)
PLANT HARDINESS ZONES: All zones as annual
ULTIMATE SIZE: 1' tall and wide
BLOOM TIME: Summer to autumn
SUN REQUIREMENT: Full sun

Native to Peru, heliotrope produces showy blooms in shades of purple, lavender, pink, and white and has thick, highly textured, dark green leaves. Some varieties are more fragrant than others, with some said to smell like cherry pie, others like vanilla. Heliotrope grows well in rich, moist soil and should be fertilized often. If you are starting from seed, sow the seeds in sandy soil about 10 weeks before outdoor planting.

7. SCENTED GERANIUM (*Pelargonium* spp.)

CLASSIFICATION: Annual (perennial in warm climates)
PLANT HARDINESS ZONES: All zones as annual
ULTIMATE SIZE: 12"–36" tall and wide
BLOOM TIME: Summer
SUN REQUIREMENT: Full sun

Related to the big red and pink geraniums of window box fame, these cousins make up for their lack of flower power with incredible fragrances ranging from lemon to chocolate to rose. Other popular types are mint, lime, orange, apple, and cinnamon. Some varieties tend to sprawl, making them excellent candidates for the sides of planters and for hanging baskets. Pinch the tips back as they grow to encourage bushiness. Repot this plant in autumn and find a spot for it on a sunny windowsill, where it will give off a luscious scent every time you brush past it.

SCENTED GERANIUM

'ROYAL CARPET' ALYSSUM

8. PURPLE ALYSSUM (*Lobularia maritima*)

CLASSIFICATION: Annual
PLANT HARDINESS ZONES: All zones
ULTIMATE SIZE: 2"–8" tall and to 12" wide
BLOOM TIME: Late spring to autumn
SUN REQUIREMENT: Full sun to partial shade

Note that this is the same easy-to-grow annual as used for number 4, but I'm specifying a purple cultivar for this part of the plan. Sow seeds directly into the soil after frost danger, or plant seeds indoors 6 to 8 weeks before transplanting outdoors. You can also purchase alyssum in flats. Deadhead to promote further flowering.

GOOD ALYSSUM CULTIVARS

'Snow Crystals'—white, with neat blooms • 'New Carpet of Snow'—white, compact form • 'Rosie O'Day'—rose-colored • 'Royal Carpet'—purple • 'Easter Bonnet' series—violet, lavender, dark pink, dark rose, white, mix, pastel mix • 'Wonderland' series—purple, lavender, pink, rose, white, mix

9. STAR GAZER LILY

(*Lilium* 'Star Gazer')

CLASSIFICATION: Bulb
PLANT HARDINESS ZONES: 3 to 8
ULTIMATE SIZE: To 18" tall and 12" wide
BLOOM TIME: Summer
SUN REQUIREMENT: Full sun

This magnificent lily has deep rose petals with dark markings, and will bloom from early to late summer. On the plan, I've indicated this plant with dotted circles, to indicate that it should be set out once it's blooming and removed after it has finished, as the stalks themselves are not ornamental. Once the lily is finished blooming, set the pot in an out-of-the-way spot; you can remove dead flowers but don't cut back stems and foliage until they have turned yellow, and continue watering. Protect the pot in winter by placing it against a sheltering wall and nestling it among bags of dried leaves.

'STAR GAZER' LILY

A HOT COLOR GARDEN

This dazzling container garden combines hot pinks, reds, and purples, along with pure yellows, to create an icy-hot vignette. Designed to be informal, even somewhat whimsical, this garden belies the careful thought that goes into mixing these steamy colors. When choosing the plants for this design, take extra care to select reds that tend toward blue rather than those that tend toward orange. Note that I've left much of the individual color choice up to you, because there is so much color variation even among plants of the same cultivar.

All of these flowers are sun-lovers, so make sure to site the garden in a sunny spot. Most of the plants in this garden are annuals. You can start many of them indoors from seed 6 to 12 weeks before planting outdoors, or you can start the seeds directly in the pots outdoors, once the weather has warmed and all danger of frost has passed. Plant nasturtium seeds outdoors after frost danger, as they don't transplant well. Once the plants have filled out, you'll have bright and lively blooms all summer long. Autumn cleanup in a garden of annuals is also very easy—just pull the plants up once they've been killed by a hard frost and throw them out. The dahlia will overwinter.

PLANTING THE HOT COLOR GARDEN, STEP BY STEP

Step 1: Begin with the largest container, which features celosia, geraniums, verbena, ivy geraniums, and dahlias. Add a layer of drainage material—either broken crockery, gravel, or 2 inches worth of Styrofoam peanuts—to the bottom of the pot, then fill the container with potting soil to within about 2 inches of the rim. Plant the dahlia bulbs about 1 inch deep and mark the spot with a golf tee or a popsicle stick so that you don't disturb them as you install the other plants. Set each plant (in its container) on top of the soil according to the garden plan, rearranging, if necessary, until you are satisfied with the way the pot looks. Use a trowel to excavate a hole for each plant, and one by one, gently remove each plant from its container, set it into its hole, and firm the soil around the plant. When you are finished installing all the plants, water well and fill in with additional soil if needed.

Step 2: Next, plant the square container, which will hold marigolds and nasturtiums. Layer drainage material on the bottom of the pot and then fill to about 2 inches from the rim with potting soil. The marigold seeds may be either started indoors from seed several weeks before

YOU WILL NEED...

* 3 containers (1 large round, 1 oval, and 1 square or rectangular, though these shapes can be altered)

* Drainage material—broken crockery, gravel, or Styrofoam peanuts

* Potting soil

* Fertilizer

* A trowel

PLANT LIST

1. Celosia (*Celosia* spp.)

2. French marigold (*Tagetes patula*)

3. Nasturtium (*Tropaeolum majus*)

4. Geranium (*Geranium* spp.)

5. Verbena (*Verbena* spp.)

6. Ivy geranium (*Pelargonium peltatum*)

7. Zinnia (*Zinnia* spp.)

8. Dahlia (*Dahlia* spp.)

A HOT COLOR GARDEN

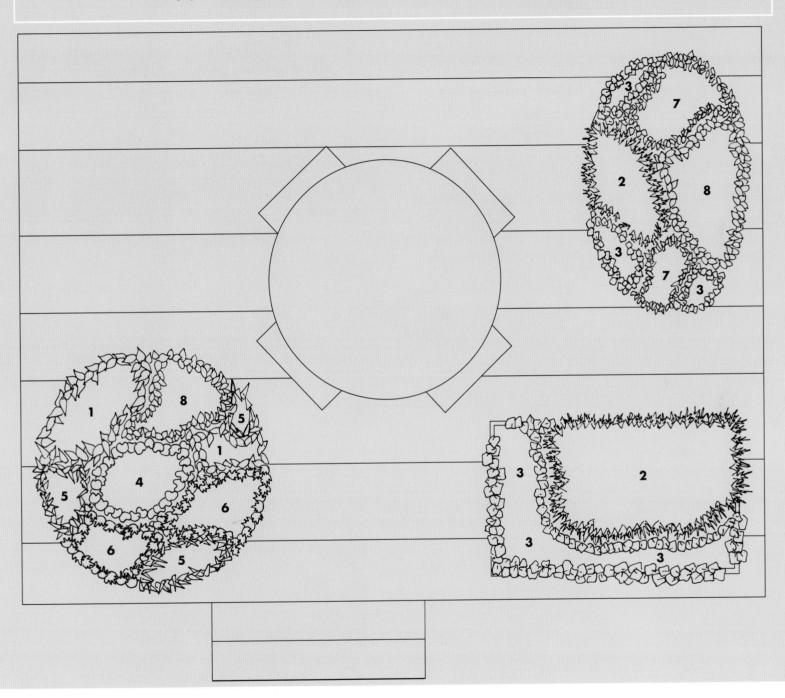

planting outdoors, or you may purchase plants in cell packs. Position the plants throughout the back and sides of the container, as shown in the plan. Sow the nasturtium seeds directly into the soil (they don't transplant very well) around the edges of the container, where they will spill over the sides as they grow. Once all the plants and seeds are in place, water gently.

Step 3: Finally, plant the container that features marigolds, nasturtiums, zinnias, and dahlias. Prepare the container with drainage material and potting soil, then plant the dahlia bulbs 1 inch deep, as in Step 1, again marking the spot with a golf tee or a stick. Install the marigolds and zinnias according to the plan, by digging small holes, setting the plants in the holes, and firming soil around them. Sow the nasturtium seeds near the edges of the container, as shown on the plan. Once all plants and seeds are in place, water well.

A NOTE ABOUT THE POTS

Because the eye-catching flowers in this garden provide a riot of color, select containers that won't compete for attention. Ceramic planters with a dark green glaze, unassuming terra-cotta pots, or simple wooden planters—all would be appropriate choices. As with all containers, make sure that there is a drainage hole in the bottom of the pot.

CALENDAR OF CARE

SPRING: *If you choose to start seeds indoors, plant them 6 to 12 weeks before you intend to install the garden outdoors; follow the directions on individual seed packets. Plant the garden outdoors after all danger of frost has passed, using either seedlings from seeds started indoors, seeds sown directly into the soil, or plants purchased in flats from a nursery.*

SUMMER: *Water the garden every day in hot, dry weather and fertilize every three weeks, according to directions on product label. Deadhead the passed flowers of annuals to promote further bloom. Pinch back the nasturtiums in midsummer to encourage fuller growth.*

AUTUMN: *If you want to enjoy the geraniums indoors in winter, remove them before a killing frost and repot. Bring indoors or into a greenhouse. As the estimated first frost date draws near, dig up the dahlia tubers, set in a cool, dry place and allow to dry. Remove spent foliage and stems. Store dried tubers in peat moss, saw dust, or shredded newspaper in a cool, dry place. Some people choose to treat dahlias like annuals, and simply start over with new ones the following year. Discard or compost other annuals after a killing frost.*

WINTER: *Clean the pots and store them in a frost-free environment, such as the basement or an attached garage.*

GETTING TO KNOW THE PLANTS

'CASTLE YELLOW' CELOSIA

I. CELOSIA (*Celosia* spp.)

CLASSIFICATION: Annual
PLANT HARDINESS ZONES: All zones
ULTIMATE SIZE: 6"–24" tall and 6"–12" wide
BLOOM TIME: Summer to autumn
SUN REQUIREMENT: Full sun

These unusual-looking annuals bear flowers that look like feathery plumes in shades of yellow, red, orange, bright pink, and purple. Plant seeds outdoors after all danger of frost has passed (they like warm soil), or start them indoors 4 weeks from the time you intend to plant outdoors. Cover seeds only lightly with soil, as light aids germination. You can also purchase celosia in flats; make sure to choose only green seedlings.

2. FRENCH MARIGOLD (*Tagetes patula*)

CLASSIFICATION: Annual
PLANT HARDINESS ZONES: All zones
ULTIMATE SIZE: To 12" tall and wide
BLOOM TIME: Summer to autumn
SUN REQUIREMENT: Full sun to partial shade

These cheerful bloomers in shades of yellow, gold, orange, and crimson will keep your pots looking good all summer long. They are also notoriously easy to grow— pretty much all they need is adequate moisture. The scent is intense, and disliked by some. Marigolds have long been used as companion plantings, as they are reputed to repel insects, though these claims have been disputed by scientists. Seeds can be sown indoors (follow seed packet directions), or can be purchased in flats.

'DISCO YELLOW' FRENCH MARIGOLD

3. NASTURTIUM

(*Tropaeolum majus*)

CLASSIFICATION: Annual
PLANT HARDINESS ZONES: All zones
ULTIMATE SIZE: 1'–8' tall, depending
　　on type, and 2' wide
BLOOM TIME: Summer
SUN REQUIREMENT: Full sun

There are many different varieties of nasturtiums: some can climb to 8 feet tall, while others remain compact, or trail only a few feet out of the container. Read the description of the particular cultivar you are buying to make sure it is suitable for a container. The blooms are red, orange, or yellow flowers, and both the flowers and their buds are edible. Use them in salads for a delightful visual treat and an intriguing peppery flavor. Sow the seeds directly in the soil after frost danger, as they don't transplant well.

'ALASKA' NASTURTIUM

'SASSY' GERANIUM

4. GERANIUM   (Pelargonium x hortorum)

CLASSIFICATION: Annual
PLANT HARDINESS ZONES: All zones
ULTIMATE SIZE: To 18" tall and 12" wide
BLOOM TIME: Late spring to autumn
SUN REQUIREMENT: Full sun to partial shade

These are the classic geraniums for bedding, containers, and hanging baskets. Though they come in shades of pink, salmon, and white, choose a vibrant red for this garden. Geraniums are undemanding to grow; they just need regular watering and fertilizing. Deadhead blooms as they fade to promote fresh flowering. The seeds can be started indoors 8 to 12 weeks or so before you plan to plant outdoors, or plants can be purchased in flats.

5. VERBENA *(Verbena* spp.)

CLASSIFICATION: Annual
PLANT HARDINESS ZONES: All zones
ULTIMATE SIZE: 1' tall and 1'–2' wide
BLOOM TIME: Summer
SUN REQUIREMENT: Full sun

This sweetly fragrant annual, with its small flower clusters and attractive dark green foliage, has a pleasing mounded form that is perfect for container culture. Flowers may be rich purple, red, or white—deadhead them as they fade to promote further bloom. Purchase seedlings in flats, or start seeds indoors 4 to 6 weeks before last frost date. Make sure to set the seeds in a dark place or to cover the seeds with black plastic, as they germinate in darkness.

'BLUE PRINCESS' VERBENA

'MANET' IVY GERANIUM

6. IVY GERANIUM *(Pelargonium peltatum)*

CLASSIFICATION: Annual
PLANT HARDINESS ZONES: All zones
ULTIMATE SIZE: 2'–4' tall and wide
BLOOM TIME: Summer
SUN REQUIREMENT: Full sun to partial shade

Like other geraniums, ivy geranium is rewarding to grow because it is both beautiful and easy to care for. Trailing tendrils reach over the sides of pots, softening the overall appearance of the garden, while long-blooming flowers in shades of magenta, red, pink, white, or lavender contribute season-long color. Fertilize and water regularly, and dead-head blooms when flowers have faded. You can start ivy geraniums from seed indoors, about 8 to 12 weeks before they are to be planted outdoors, or purchase them in cells from a nursery.

ZINNIAS

7. ZINNIA (*Zinnia* spp.)

CLASSIFICATION: Annual
PLANT HARDINESS ZONES: All zones
ULTIMATE SIZE: 6"–3' tall and
    6"–8" wide
BLOOM TIME: Midsummer through
    autumn
SUN REQUIREMENT: Full sun

Zinnias come in a range of bold colors, including yellows, oranges, and reds, as well as more pastel shades. For this garden, elect to use one of the bright shades. Flowers may be single (with petals arranged in one row around the center) or double (with multiple layers of petals around the flower center); choose the type you like best. Sow the seeds directly in the container after all danger of frost, or purchase zinnias in flats. These flowers need good air circulation, so make sure to space them 12 inches apart. Water the plant at the soil level, keeping the leaves dry, to help prevent disease.

HOT-COLORED ZINNIAS
- 'Small World Cherry'—bright pink
- 'Scarlet Splendor'—vivid red
- 'Canary Bird'—bright yellow
- 'Benary's Giant Mix'—a mix of clear yellow, orange, white, red, magenta
- 'Dreamland' series—comes in scarlet, pink, and a mix of these two colors, plus yellow, white, and orange

8. DAHLIA (*Dahlia* spp.)

CLASSIFICATION: Bulb (tuber)
PLANT HARDINESS ZONES: All zones
   (8 to 10 for overwintering)
ULTIMATE SIZE: 1'–4' tall and
   6"–12" wide
BLOOM TIME: Summer til frost
SUN REQUIREMENT: Full sun

Dahlias have large, highly ornamental blooms that come in a wide array of sizes, colors, and shapes (in fact, there are eleven different categories of dahlias). Because there are so many different types, read the description for the cultivar you are considering carefully. They are generally grown from tubers, which should be planted in early spring. Native to Mexico, dahlias are tender and will not overwinter in the ground above Zone 8, but you can lift them and store them indoors, to be replanted the next season.

'MOONFIRE' DAHLIA

A SHADY GARDEN

Not every garden is showered with six hours of sun a day, and more and more, gardeners are coming to recognize the blessings of shade. A shady retreat—whether it's on a porch, in a corner of a terrace, or under the canopy of a large shade tree—is a wonderful asset on a hot summer day. A potted garden for a shady spot requires a different "vocabulary" of plants than one grown in sun, and these shady gardens are likely to be a bit more subtle than their full-sun cousins. But subtle doesn't mean plain or boring. The garden design shown here offers a variety of colors, heights, shapes, and textures—all the features of a successful planting scheme—while making use of a combination of perennials, including hostas, ferns, and bleeding hearts, as well as annuals or tender perennials like fuchsia, New Guinea impatiens, coleus, and sweet potato vine.

The garden is depicted in the corner of a shady patio, but you could move the containers about to suit any number of situations. Plant this garden in spring, after danger of frost has passed. You may wish to start the seeds of annuals indoors.

PLANTING THE SHADY GARDEN, STEP BY STEP

Step 1: Make sure to position your planters where they will ultimately be sited. The large trough-style planters, in particular, will be too heavy to move once they are filled with soil and plants.

Step 2: Prepare the trough-style planter that will hold the hosta, caladium, coleus, fuchsia, ivy, and sweet potato vine by layering drainage material—either broken shards of crockery, gravel, or Styrofoam peanuts—on the bottom. Then, fill the trough about two-thirds full with potting mix. Set the plants in their containers on top of the soil, according to the garden plan; rearrange if necessary, until you are satisfied with the design. Gently remove a plant from its container, dig a small hole, set the plant in the hole, and firm soil around the base. Continue installing the plants one by one until all are in place, filling in with additional soil as needed. Water well, then add more soil if necessary.

Step 3: Next, plant the trough-style planter that features Japanese painted fern, wild bleeding heart, coleus, New Guinea impatiens, ivy, and sweet potato vine. Prepare the container and install the plants as in Step 2.

YOU WILL NEED...

- 6 planters—4 large pots and 2 trough-style planters, if you are following the plan exactly

- Drainage material—broken crockery, gravel, or Styrofoam peanuts

- Potting soil

- Fertilizer

- A trowel

PLANT LIST

1. Hosta (*Hosta* spp.)

2. Japanese painted fern (*Athyrium nipponicum* 'Pictum')

3. Wild bleeding heart (*Dicentra eximia*)

4. Caladium (*Caladium* spp.)

5. Coral bells (*Heuchera* spp.)

6. Boston fern (*Nephrolepis exaltata* 'Bostoniensis')

7. Coleus (*Coleus* spp.)

8. New Guinea impatiens (*Impatiens* x *hawkeri*)

9. Fuchsia (*Fuchsia* spp.)

10. Variegated ivy (*Hedera* spp.)

11. Sweet potato vine (*Ipomoea batatas*)

A SHADY GARDEN

Step 4: Prepare the container that will hold wild bleeding heart, caladium, fuchsia, and sweet potato vine by layering the bottom with drainage material. Fill the container with potting soil to about 2 or 3 inches below the rim. Remove the plants one by one and install them according to the garden plan, making adjustments where necessary. Water well and add potting soil if needed.

Step 5: The pot that features Japanese painted fern, wild bleeding heart, coral bells, and sweet potato vine comes next. Plant all as for Step 4, making sure to place the coral bells—the tallest plant—in the middle.

Step 6: Plant the hostas and ivy in the fifth container, first preparing the pot as you did the others. Be sure to place the ivy near the edge of the container, where it will trail attractively over the sides.

Step 7: Finally, plant the Boston ferns in the last container. Water all plants well.

CALENDAR OF CARE

SPRING: *Plant the garden in spring, after all danger of frost has passed. In following springs, you will need to check on any perennials that have been overwintered in pots. Discard those that have not done well. Fertilize those that have survived. Clean stored pots and prepare them for planting. Start seeds for coleus indoors, according to the instructions on the seed packet.*

SUMMER: *Water as needed—daily in hot weather—and fertilize every three weeks. Deadhead fuchsia, bleeding heart, and New Guinea impatiens as flowers fade, to promote further flowering. Pinch back coleus flower buds as they form to encourage foliage growth, and periodically pinch back the vines of the sweet potato to promote a fuller, bushier habit.*

AUTUMN: *Before the first frost, repot the sweet potato vine and bring it indoors to enjoy as a houseplant through the winter. Alternatively, take cuttings to root in glasses of water on your windowsill, and treat the plant as an annual. Cut back dead foliage of the perennials and move the pots to a sheltering wall (be sure to buy weather-resistant pots for your perennials). Protect the pots by nestling them among bags filled with dried leaves. Pull out dead annuals and discard or compost them.*

WINTER: *Clean and store any remaining pots indoors for the winter.*

GETTING TO KNOW THE PLANTS

'ELEGANS' HOSTA

I. HOSTA (*Hosta* spp.)

CLASSIFICATION: Perennial
PLANT HARDINESS ZONES: 3 to 8
ULTIMATE SIZE: 6"–3' tall and 1'–4' wide, depending on species
BLOOM TIME: Summer
SUN REQUIREMENT: Partial shade to full shade

Hostas are a favorite with home gardeners, for their stalwart dependability and their ornamental foliage, which ranges from dark green to bluish green to gold-green and cream-and-green variegations, depending on the species and cultivar you select. In addition to its interesting foliage colors, hostas feature rich texture, including some with a seersucker effect. In summer, tall flower stalks in shades of lavender or white rise above the leaves. Read the description carefully and choose one of the smaller cultivars, as some can get quite large and unwieldy in a container. Hostas are widely available at local nurseries and garden centers, but you may also wish to peruse the offerings from mail-order nurseries, which tend to feature more variety.

SMALL HOSTAS FOR CONTAINERS

'Dorset Blue'—rounded, bluish leaves and white flowers • 'Gold Edger'—gold-colored foliage • 'Patriot'—dark green leaves with white edging • 'Brim Cup'—highly textured leaves with a white margin • 'Summer Music'—leaves with a white center and gold-green edging

2. JAPANESE PAINTED FERN
(*Athyrium nipponicum* 'Pictum')

CLASSIFICATION: Fern
PLANT HARDINESS ZONES: 3 to 9
ULTIMATE SIZE: 12"–18" tall and wide
BLOOM TIME: Insignificant
SUN REQUIREMENT: Partial to full shade

Perfect for brightening a shady spot, this beautiful fern has deep red stems and green fronds accented with a silver steak, hence its common name. It is also easy to care for, requiring only regular watering and rich, well-drained soil (which is easy to achieve in a container). It will thrive in almost any type of shade.

JAPANESE PAINTED FERN

WILD BLEEDING HEART

3. WILD BLEEDING HEART (*Dicentra eximia*)

CLASSIFICATION: Perennial
PLANT HARDINESS ZONES: 4 to 9
ULTIMATE SIZE: 8"–15" tall and 12"–18" wide
BLOOM TIME: Spring through autumn
SUN REQUIREMENT: Partial shade

Wild bleeding heart (*Dicentra eximia*) is perhaps a bit more difficult to find than the common bleeding heart (*Dicentra spectabilis*), but worth searching for because of its long flowering period. In fact, it is one of the longest flowering perennials for shade, blooming profusely in spring, tapering off a bit in the heat of summer, but picking up again as the weather cools. In addition, its finely cut leaves remain attractive throughout the season. The flowers range from light pink to deep rose, and are shaped like small hearts. If you can't locate wild bleeding heart, by all means plant common bleeding heart—the flowers are even more charming, but generally last only for several weeks in spring.

'AARON' CALADIUM

4. CALADIUM (*Caladium* spp.)

CLASSIFICATION: Bulb
PLANT HARDINESS ZONES: 9 to 11 for overwintering outdoors
ULTIMATE SIZE: 1'–2' tall and 1' wide
BLOOM TIME: Insignificant
SUN REQUIREMENT: Partial shade

Caladiums are grown for their large, highly ornamental leaves, available in a range of colors, from pink to red to white to green, including some bicolors and multicolors. They like a warm, moist climate, and should be exposed only to filtered sun (direct sunlight can "burn" the leaves). Because of their tropical nature, caladiums need to be brought indoors to live as houseplants or overwintered as bulbs. Some gardeners treat them as expensive annuals, discarding them at the end of the season and purchasing new ones the following spring. (Caladium bulbs can take 8 weeks to get started, so start them indoors or be patient!)

5. CORAL BELLS   (*Heuchera* spp.)

CLASSIFICATION: Perennial
PLANT HARDINESS ZONES: 3 to 9
ULTIMATE SIZE: 18" tall and wide
BLOOM TIME: Early to midsummer
SUN REQUIREMENT: Sun to partial shade

Slender flower stalks bearing bell-shaped blooms rise above neat mounds of foliage. Cultivars in an array of colors are available, from pink to red to white. Cut back spent flower stalks to encourage further bloom. This plant is easy to grow as long as you provide excellent drainage. It is hardy to Zone 3, so should survive most winters with some protection.

'EBONY AND IVORY' CORAL BELLS

BOSTON FERN

6. BOSTON FERN   (*Nephrolepis exaltata* 'Bostoniensis')

CLASSIFICATION: Fern
PLANT HARDINESS ZONES: 8 to 11 for overwintering
ULTIMATE SIZE: 18" to 36" tall and 36" to 60" wide
BLOOM TIME: Insignificant
SUN REQUIREMENT: Partial shade

Boston ferns will thrive in drier soil and more light than most other ferns, which has made them popular houseplants. Site your container of Boston ferns where light is bright but filtered. This plant dislikes wet leaves, so mist it only when the weather is hot enough to dry the foliage quickly (about an hour). Otherwise, confine your watering to the soil level, and feed the plant once a month with diluted liquid fertilizer. When the weather turns cool, bring your Boston ferns into the house, where they will live happily all winter.

'Queen Victoria' coleus

7. COLEUS (*Coleus* spp.)

CLASSIFICATION: Annual
PLANT HARDINESS ZONES: All zones
ULTIMATE SIZE: 10" tall and wide
BLOOM TIME: Insignificant
SUN REQUIREMENT: Partial to full shade

With its variable and showy leaf forms and colors, coleus is a tried-and-true annual for the shady garden. Leaves range from red to purple to lime green to salmon to bright pink, with many cultivars having more than one color on each leaf. There are smooth-edged and scalloped leaves, heart-shaped ones and lance-shaped ones, large and small, with almost infinite variety. Coleus is easy to grow from seed, or you can purchase them in flats. Pinch back the plants when they are young to encourage a bushy habit and pinch off the tiny flowers. Partial shade is best, as the leaves get enough light to develop vibrant colors but not enough to bleach them.

8. NEW GUINEA IMPATIENS

(*Impatiens* x *hawkeri*)

CLASSIFICATION: Annual
PLANT HARDINESS ZONES: All zones
ULTIMATE SIZE: 18" tall and wide
BLOOM TIME: Late spring to autumn
SUN REQUIREMENT: Full sun to partial shade

New Guinea impatiens is a terrific plant for containers, where its large flowers (in colors from lavender, bright purple, and pink to red, orange, and salmon) and its bold, often variegated, leaves draw plenty of attention. This plant does best in lighter shade (morning sun and afternoon shade is ideal), so if your site is very shady, substitute busy lizzies (*Impatiens wallerana*), which look similar but tolerate deeper shade. They are easy to care for, requiring regular watering and only light fertilizing. Buy these plants in flats, as most types are propagated from tip cuttings rather than seed.

NEW GUINEA IMPATIENS

'MRS. MARSHALL' FUCHSIA

9. FUCHSIA   (*Fuchsia* spp.)

CLASSIFICATION: Shrub
PLANT HARDINESS ZONES: Annual in all zones; perennial in 10 to 11
ULTIMATE SIZE: 12"–24" tall and 24"–36" wide
BLOOM TIME: Late spring to early autumn
SUN REQUIREMENT: Partial shade

Fuchsia's two-toned, pendant flowers are well loved by gardeners for the flash of bright color—red, purple, pink, coral, or white—they offer shady spots. The trailing varieties (as opposed to the upright-growing ones) are best for containers, so read the plant description before you buy. Mist plants in hot weather, in addition to regular watering. Fuchsias will need to be moved to a frost-free location in winter, ideally to a sunroom or heated porch, since they are tender plants and will not overwinter outdoors except in zones 10 and 11.

VARIEGATED IVY

10. VARIEGATED IVY
(*Hedera* spp.)

CLASSIFICATION: Perennial
PLANT HARDINESS ZONES: All zones if
   wintered indoors; 8 to 10 outdoors
ULTIMATE SIZE: 6"–12" tall and
   spreading
BLOOM TIME: None
SUN REQUIREMENT: Partial shade

Variegated ivies are somewhat less
hardy than the straight green species,
but all are easy to care for. Ivy can be
found at garden centers and nurseries
in small containers; you can propagate
additional plants from cuttings. At the
end of the growing season, cut several
tendrils from the plans and root them
in water or moist sand. Keep them
indoors, and you should have viable
plants in about a year. In cold climates,
remove ivy before a killing frost and
repot it. Bring the plant indoors for the
winter, and reuse it the following spring.

'BLACKIE' AND 'MARGARITA' SWEET POTATO VINE

11. SWEET POTATO VINE   (*Ipomoea batatas*)

CLASSIFICATION: Perennial
PLANT HARDINESS ZONES: 6 to 9
ULTIMATE SIZE: 18" tall and 24" wide
BLOOM TIME: Summer
SUN REQUIREMENT: Full sun to partial shade

This South American native is widely grown for its edible tubers, though there are also many types grown purely for their ornamental foliage, which ranges from lime green to deep purple, depending upon the variety. Pinch back the vines if they become too long, or to encourage bushiness. Because it is native to the southern hemisphere, it is not surprising that sweet potato vine does best where summers are long and warm; it is best brought indoors for the winter (or regrown the next year), as it is unlikely to overwinter successfully in pots, except in the southernmost regions of the United States. While most garden references recommend this as a plant for full sun, it also performs well in partial shade. You can start sweet potato vine by suspending a sweet potato skewered with toothpicks set on top of a water-filled glass (as you might have done in elementary school gardening experiments), but you can also purchase ornamental varieties and nurseries and garden centers. Putting cuttings of an existing plant into a glass will also work.

A WINDOW BOX GARDEN

Lush flowers and greenery flowing out of cheery window boxes provide the perfect finishing detail for any home, whether it's a country cottage, a stately brownstone, or a traditional house in the suburbs. There are many styles of window boxes available to suit various types of homes, including classic painted wooden boxes, terra-cotta troughs, "antiqued" planters, and boxes made of fiberglass and other modern materials that mimic the look of wood or stone.

If you are planting large window boxes, it is probably best to set them in place on the windowsills before you begin planting. If the box will be affixed to a wall outside the window, this must, of course, be done before the box is filled. Note that some gardeners prefer to plant their flowers and foliage in separate pots and simply set the pots inside the window box. If your window box is small, or if you are planning to plant in separate containers, you can pot everything up outdoors.

Creating pleasing combinations for the upper stories of a home requires a different perspective—the window box gardens in this plan are designed to be attractive both from the ground and through the windows.

PLANTING THE WINDOW BOX GARDEN, STEP BY STEP

Step 1: If your window boxes must be installed on a wall before planting, do this first, making sure they are well secured. If you are planting from the interior, drape heavy plastic over your sill, walls, and floor to protect them from any stray potting material.

Step 2: Prepare the window box that will be filled with geraniums, helichrysum, heliotrope, and scaevola by layering drainage material to a depth of 2 inches along the bottom. Fill the trough about two thirds of the way to the top with potting mix. Arrange the plants in the trough according to the design, making adjustments as necessary. Once you are satisfied with the design, remove the plants from their cells one by one, set them on the soil, and fill in around them with additional soil, firming around the base of the plant. Begin with the part of the container furthest from you, and work forward. When all plants are installed, water well and add more soil if necessary.

Step 3: Following the instructions as for Steps 1 and 2, prepare and plant the window box that will hold verbena, lobelia, helichrysum, and African daisies. Note that you

YOU WILL NEED...

- Window boxes (2 trough-style window boxes and 1 hayrack style window box, if you are planting the design exactly)

- Coco-fiber liner (for hayrack-style window box)

- Hardware for affixing the window boxes to the house (or porch railings)

- Drainage material—broken crockery, gravel, or Styrofoam peanuts

- Potting soil

- Fertilizer

- A trowel

- A watering can (you will most likely need to water these planters from inside your house)

- Heavy plastic (such as garbage bags) to protect interior floors from potting materials

PLANT LIST

1. Geranium (*Pelargonium* spp.)

2. Verbena (*Verbena* spp.)

3. Lobelia (*Lobelia erinus*)

4. Helichrysum (*Helichrysum petiolatum*)

5. Heliotrope (*Heliotropium* spp.)

6. Scaevola (*Scaevola* spp.)

7. African daisy (*Arctotis stoechadifolia*)

A WINDOW BOX GARDEN

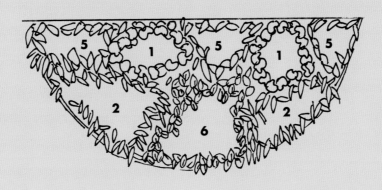

can plant the African daisy seeds directly in the soil if you like; just make sure that all danger of frost has passed.

Step 4: Line the hayrack planter with the coco-fiber liner. Most companies that produce hayracks also sell coco-fiber liners made to fit. Because the coco-fiber liner itself is porous and drains freely, you will not need to layer drainage material in the bottom of this planter. Fill it about two-thirds full with potting mix, and install the plants according to the design. Water well and fill with additional soil if necessary.

WINDOW BOX VARIATIONS

Once you've gotten the hang of planting window boxes, you can experiment with different themes. Here are a few good ones to try:

* Plant culinary herbs at a kitchen window.
* Set highly scented plants at a window kept open in summer.
* Plant miniature boxwood or tiny Alberta spruce for winter displays.
* Create a spring scene with miniature daffodils and trailing ivy.

CONTAINERS FOR WINDOWSILLS

When decorating your windowsills with plants, you needn't confine yourself to the standard rectangular wooden box. Particularly if you have wide sills that can accommodate a large container, you can adapt all manner of receptacles for this use (always be sure that the container can be anchored securely—you don't want the container falling off the ledge in a heavy wind). It's best if you can drill holes in your container, but if you can't, add plenty of drainage material to the bottom of the pot. Consider using one of the following for containers, or use your imagination to create a one-of-a kind planter.

* An oval galvanized metal tub
* A series of same-size ceramic or terracotta pots
* A large wooden garden trug
* A picnic hamper
* A painted wooden planter decorated with stencilling

CALENDAR OF CARE

SPRING: *Install new window boxes. Check to be sure existing window boxes are securely attached. If you had winter plantings that you are replacing, remove any dead plant material and debris. Add potting soil as necessary. Plant this garden in spring, after all danger of frost has passed. You may wish to start seeds of annuals indoors 4 to 12 weeks before planting outdoors; follow the instructions on individual seed packets.*

SUMMER: *Water window boxes regularly; this may mean daily in hot, dry weather. Fertilize every three weeks, following instructions on fertilizer label. Pinch back tips of geraniums as needed to encourage bushiness. Cut helichrysum back after flowering, to keep it neat. Deadhead annuals as needed.*

AUTUMN: *Before first frost, repot geraniums and helichrysum and move indoors, if desired. Remove and discard dead plants after a killing frost. Detach window boxes from their mountings for winter storage (unless you plan winter displays). Remove the soil and clean the boxes thoroughly. Check walls and sills behind and under window boxes for possible damage (rot can be a problem over time if the area retains moisture).*

WINTER: *Repair and repaint wooden window boxes, as necessary.*

GETTING TO KNOW THE PLANTS

'MAIDEN ROSE PINK' GERANIUM

1. GERANIUM   (*Pelargonium* spp.)

CLASSIFICATION: Annual (perennial in warm climates)
PLANT HARDINESS ZONES: All zones as annual
ULTIMATE SIZE: 12"–36" tall and wide
BLOOM TIME: Summer
SUN REQUIREMENT: Full sun

These geraniums are related to the big red and pink "zonal" geraniums so familiar in window boxes and other containers. While the blooms are more subtle than their showy cousins, they exude a charm all their own. Some varieties tend to sprawl, making them excellent candidates for the sides of planters and for hanging baskets. Pinch the tips back as they grow if you want to encourage bushiness. Repot this plant in autumn and find a spot for it on a windowsill, where it will cheer a sunny room all winter.

2. VERBENA   (*Verbena* spp.)

CLASSIFICATION: Annual
PLANT HARDINESS ZONES: All zones
ULTIMATE SIZE: 1' tall and 1'–2' wide
BLOOM TIME: Summer
SUN REQUIREMENT: Full sun

Planted for its sweet perfume, as well as for its appealing small flower clusters and luscious dark green foliage, verbena's low, mounded habit has made it a favorite for window boxes and other containers. Flowers may be rich purple, red, or white—deadhead them as they fade to promote further bloom. Purchase seedlings in flats, or start seeds indoors 4 to 6 weeks before last frost date. Make sure to set the seeds in a dark place or to cover the seeds with black plastic, as they germinate in darkness.

'WHITE HECTOR' VERBENA

'CRYSTAL PALACE' LOBELIA

3. LOBELIA   (*Lobelia erinus*)

CLASSIFICATION: Annual
PLANT HARDINESS ZONES: All zones
ULTIMATE SIZE: 6" tall and wide
BLOOM TIME: Late spring til autumn
SUN REQUIREMENT: Full sun to partial shade

Lobelia is well-loved for its long bloom period, its cascading habit, and its lovely flowers, which come in masses of small blue, white, pink, purple, or red blooms. This annual performs best in cooler climates; if you live where summers are hot, make sure to give lobelia partial shade. Deadhead or cut back as blooms fade to promote reflowering. You can start lobelia from seed or purchase plants in flats.

'LIMELIGHT' HELICHRYSUM

4. HELICHRYSUM (*Helichrysum petiolatum*)

CLASSIFICATION: Annual, perennial in warm climates
PLANT HARDINESS ZONES: All zones as annual
ULTIMATE SIZE: 8"–10" (trailing) and 12" wide
BLOOM TIME: Grown for foliage
SUN REQUIREMENT: Sun to partial shade

Helichrysum, also called licorice plant, is actually a tender perennial, but will not overwinter above zones 10 and 11, so is treated as an annual throughout most of the continent. Its sprawling growth habit makes it ideal for containers, particularly window boxes and hanging baskets. Leaves are velvety in texture, and are the reason for growing this plant, as the flowers are insignificant. Cut the plant back after it flowers to keep it looking neat. If you like, you can repot helichrysum and overwinter it indoors.

'GRUNEWALD SELECT' HELIOTROPE

5. HELIOTROPE (*Heliotropium* spp.)

CLASSIFICATION: Annual (perennial in warm climates)
PLANT HARDINESS ZONES: All zones as annual
ULTIMATE SIZE: 1' tall and wide
BLOOM TIME: Summer to autumn
SUN REQUIREMENT: Full sun

Heliotrope's small clusters of blooms are heavily fragrant, with a scent that is often describes as vanilla-like. It is free-flowering, with blossoms in shades of purple as well as in white, and is very attractive to butterflies. This shrubby plant likes lots of sun and water, and should be fertilized regularly. If you are starting from seed, sow the seeds in sandy soil about 10 weeks before outdoor planting. Otherwise, purchase at a garden center or nursery and plant after all danger of frost has passed.

6. SCAEVOLA (*Scaevola* spp.)

CLASSIFICATION: Annual
PLANT HARDINESS ZONES: All zones
ULTIMATE SIZE: 4"–6" tall and wide
BLOOM TIME: Late spring til autumn
SUN REQUIREMENT: Full sun to partial shade

Native to Australia, scaevola likes sun (though it will do fine with some shade) and sharp drainage, and once the plant is established, it needs little watering. The flowers are an interesting shape—they look like miniature fans—and are available in white, lilac, and dusty rose-purple. Scaevola is also extremely long-flowering, lasting from late spring until a killing frost. The plant's cascading habit makes it particularly desirable for window boxes and hanging baskets. A fertilizer that contains iron sulfate will produce a deeper color in the blooms.

'BLUE WONDER' SCAEVOLA

AFRICAN DAISY

7. AFRICAN DAISY (*Arctotis stoechadifolia*)

CLASSIFICATION: Annual
PLANT HARDINESS ZONES: All zones
ULTIMATE SIZE: To 18" tall and 4' wide
BLOOM TIME: Early spring to late summer
SUN REQUIREMENT: Full sun

There are a number of different flowers all with the common name "African daisy"—this species has the namesake daisy-type flowers in shades of yellow, orange, red, purple, white, or cream, along with beautiful silvery leaves. This is definitely a plant for full sun (its flowers close at night, and may not open on cloudy days). You can sow the seeds directly into the soil after all danger of frost has passed; the seeds germinate quickly (make sure not to overwater these seeds, as they become more susceptible to disease when constantly moist).

PLANT HARDINESS ZONES

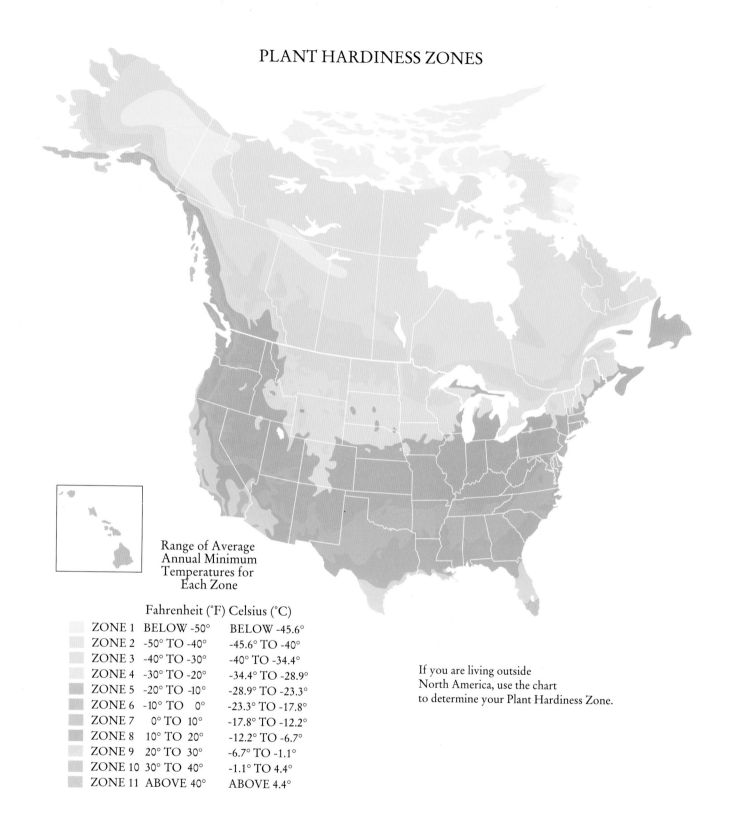

Range of Average
Annual Minimum
Temperatures for
Each Zone

	Fahrenheit (°F)	Celsius (°C)
ZONE 1	BELOW -50°	BELOW -45.6°
ZONE 2	-50° TO -40°	-45.6° TO -40°
ZONE 3	-40° TO -30°	-40° TO -34.4°
ZONE 4	-30° TO -20°	-34.4° TO -28.9°
ZONE 5	-20° TO -10°	-28.9° TO -23.3°
ZONE 6	-10° TO 0°	-23.3° TO -17.8°
ZONE 7	0° TO 10°	-17.8° TO -12.2°
ZONE 8	10° TO 20°	-12.2° TO -6.7°
ZONE 9	20° TO 30°	-6.7° TO -1.1°
ZONE 10	30° TO 40°	-1.1° TO 4.4°
ZONE 11	ABOVE 40°	ABOVE 4.4°

If you are living outside
North America, use the chart
to determine your Plant Hardiness Zone.

APPENDIX

METRIC CONVERSIONS

Throughout this book, standard American measures have been used. If you would like to convert the measures to metric measurements, use the following chart as your guide.

Length and distance

Inches x 25.4 = millimeters

Inches x 2.54 = centimeters

Feet x 30.48 = centimeters

Feet x .3048 = meters

Yards x .9144 = meters

Area

Square inches x 6.4516 = cm^2

Square feet x 929.0304 = cm^2

Square feet x .093 = m^2

Square yards x .836 = m^2

SOURCES OF INFORMATION

Garden clubs, horticultural societies, and information service providers, including websites and local agricultural extension agencies, can provide valuable information for gardeners from beginning to advanced. Check your local telephone directory for nearby garden clubs and the county extension office. Following are some websites that offer a range of helpful gardening information.

www.ivillage.com/home/garden

www.neoflora.com

www.gardenweb.com

www.garden-gate.prairienet.org

ORGANIZING YOUR POTTING PLACE

f you are planning a container garden, you will need to plant and transplant seedlings as well as larger specimens that must be installed in containers or are outgrowing their pots. This means that you will need a space to perform these tasks and an area to store your tools and supplies.

Perhaps the best solution is a potting bench, typically a counter-height worktable, often with a hutch above and drawers or bins below. A potting bench will allow you to keep all your potting accoutrements handy, and features storage for stowing bags of potting mix and fertilizer, extra plastic and terra-cotta pots, trowels and dibbles, and all the other items you'll be using.

You can site your potting bench outdoors, along a wall or in an out-of-the-way corner of your patio or deck. This will make cleanup simpler, as you won't have to worry about loose soil falling on the ground or about water getting everywhere. An outdoor site is ideal if you plan to buy most of your plants in flats at the nursery and install them in containers once the weather is more temperate. But if you'd like to start a lot of seeds indoors and expect to begin when the weather is still cold, an indoor site may be best. Because starting seeds and potting up plants can be untidy, to say the least, choose an indoor site like a basement, garage, or mudroom, where a bit of a mess won't be a problem.

You can also make your potting place a temporary affair by setting up on the kitchen table or on a picnic table outdoors. A plastic tablecloth will protect the surface and will even out a rough wood surface, such as that of a picnic table. If you are opting for a temporary spot, find a roomy garden trug or a small cart or wagon to transport your plants and supplies to your work space.

Wherever you decide to pot your plants, you'll want nearby surfaces to be wipe-clean and you'll need to be near a water source. If possible, set up within reach of a garden hose, because lugging a full watering can will take its toll on your back. You will still need the watering can if you are planting seeds or tiny seedlings, because these little plants are delicate and may be harmed by a heavy stream of water, but it will be much easier if you can fill the watering can from the hose rather than carrying the can back and forth. If you simply can't find a spot close enough to a water source, load full watering cans into a wheelbarrow or cart and roll them to your potting place. Good overhead light is a requirement for a potting area, too, so you can read directions on seed packets easily and see the tiny seeds you are sowing or the tender shoots of the seedlings you are transplanting.

Add more storage to your potting place by mounting a few hooks along the edge of your potting bench or on a nearby wall; from these hooks you can hang tools, gloves, or a small hand broom for cleaning up. The items will be within easy reach, yet they won't clutter your worktable. Large plastic bins with lids are excellent for stashing heavier items like bags of potting mix and broken shards of pottery you are saving for draingage material. Do be sure to store fertilizer and any herbicides or insecticides out of reach of children and pets, as these may be harmful if handled or swallowed. If you need to keep them near ground level, choose a cabinet with a lock or invest in a small outdoor storage unit that can be locked.

Now that you're on your way to organizing your potting area, here are some useful tips that will help you maximize your time and space:

- Look for an old dresser at a flea market or tag sale; this versatile piece can be pressed into service as a potting bench. The top can be used as a work surface and the drawers can store supplies.
- Group tools and supplies according to function. This will allow you to find what you need when you need it. Items that you use often should also be grouped together.

- Make sure to keep sharp and pointed tools together, and stored in such a way that you won't injure yourself while you're searching for them.
- Keep a garden journal and a pen handy as you pot your plants, and jot down the date and task you are performing. As the season advances, take additional dated notes. You'll be able to chart your garden's progress, and the following year you'll be able to learn from your mistakes—and your successes.
- A potting tray or "tidy" may be all you need for smaller jobs. This plastic basin has a shallow lip along the front, to prevent dirt from spilling over, and three higher sides, which keep all your supplies contained. The advantage of the potting tidy is that is is portable and can be stored in a closet, shed, or garage when not in use, yet effectively protects surfaces from water and mud.
- A tool belt, similar to those designed for carpenters, can be a useful thing as you pot up your plants. You can find one meant especially for gardeners or you may wish to adapt a true carpenter's tool belt.
- Get in the habit of cleaning your pots when you empty them, so they'll be ready when you need them.
- Store similar-size pots inside each other and place them on their sides on a shelf. This way, you can make longer stacks without fearing that they'll topple over.

SOURCES FOR PLANTS AND SUPPLIES

PLANTS

Bear Creek Nursery
P.O. Box 411
Northport, WA 99157
Specializes in cold-hardy fruit trees, shrubs, and berries.

Busse Gardens
13579 10th St. NW
Cokato, MN 55321
(612) 286-2654
Fabulous hardy perennial plants, including wildflowers, hostas, and heucheras.

Comstock Seed
8520 W. 4th St.
Reno, NV 89523
(702) 746-3681
Seed supplier for drought-tolerant native grasses and other plants of the Great Basin.

Edible Landscaping
P.O. Box 77
Afton, VA 22920
(804) 361-9134
Edible for you and the birds and other wildlife—many fruiting trees and shrubs.

Forestfarm
990 Tetherow Road
Williams, OR 97544
(503) 846-7269
Catalog of more than two thousand plants, including Western natives, perennials, and an outstanding variety of trees and shrubs.

The Fragrant Path
P.O. Box 328
Ft. Calhoun, NE 68023
Seeds for fragrant annuals, perennials, shrubs, and vines, many of them old-fashioned favorites.

Gardens of the Blue Ridge
9056 Pittman Gap Road
P.O. Box 10
Pineola, NC 28662
Excellent selection of native trees and shrubs.

Goodwin Creek Gardens
P.O. Box 83
Williams, OR 97544
(541) 846-7375
Specializes in herbs, everlasting flowers, and fragrant plants, as well as plants that attract butterflies and hummingbirds.

Holbrook Farm & Nursery
115 Lance Road
P.O. Box 368
Fletcher, NC 28732
Good selection of flowering shrubs.

Jackson & Perkins
P.O. Box 1028
Medford, OR 97501
(800) 292-4769
Fine selection of roses, perennials, and other garden-worthy plants.

J.L. Hudson, Seedsman
P.O. Box 1058
Redwood City, CA 94064
Seeds, vegetables, herbs, and heirlooms.

Johnny's Selected Seeds
Foss Hill Road
Albion, ME 04910-9731
(207) 437-9294
Grasses, heirlooms, herbs, seeds, supplies, vegetables.

Kurt Bluemel, Inc.
2740 Green Lane
Baldwin, MD 31013
Excellent selection of ornamental grasses, rushes, and sedges.

Lilypons Water Gardens
P.O. Box 10
6800 Lilypons Road
Buckeystown, MD 21717
(301) 874-5133
Plants and supplies for water gardens.

Morden Nurseries, Ltd.
P.O. Box 1270
Morden, MB
Canada R0G 1J0
Wide selection of ornamental trees and shrubs.

Niche Gardens
1111 Dawson Rd.
Chapel Hill, NC 27516
(919) 967-0078
Good, healthy plants of grasses, nursery-propagated wildflowers, perennials, and herbs.

Northwoods Nursery
27368 South Oglesby
Canby, OR 97013
(503) 266-5432
Ornamental trees, shrubs, and vines.

Prairie Moon Nursery
Rt. 3 Box 163
Winona, MN 55987
(507) 452-1362
Generously sized plants and seeds of native prairie grasses and wildflowers.

Prairie Nursery
P.O. Box 306
Westfield, WI 53964
(608) 296-3679
Catalog of prairie grasses and native wildflowers.

Santa Barbara Heirloom
  Seedling Nursery
P.O. Box 4235
Santa Barbara, CA 93140
(805) 968-5444
Organically grown heirloom seedlings of vegetables, herbs, and edible flowers.

Shady Oaks Nursery
112 10th Ave. SE
Waseca, MN 56093
(507) 835-5033
Specializes in plants that thrive in shade, including wildflowers, ferns, perennials, shrubs, and others.

Shepherd's Garden Seeds
30 Irene Street
Torrington, CT 06790
(860) 482-0532
Fine selection of annuals, perennials, vegetables, and herbs.

Southwestern Native Seeds
P.O. Box 50503
Tucson, AZ 85703
Responsibly collected wildflower seeds from the Southwest, West, and Mexico.

Sunlight Gardens
Rt. 1 Box 600-A
Hillvale Rd.
Andersonville, TN 37705
(615) 494-8237
Wonderful selection of wildflowers, all nursery propagated.

Tripple Brook Farm
37 Middle Rd.
Southampton, MA 01073
(413) 527-4626
Wildflowers and other Northeastern native plants, along with fruits and shrubs.

Van Engelen Inc.
23 Tulip Drive
Bantam, CT 06750
Wide variety of bulbs.

Van Ness Water Gardens
2460 N. Euclid Ave.
Upland, CA 91786
(909) 982-2425
Everything you could possibly need for a water garden, from plants to pools to supplies.

Vermont Wildflower Farm
Rt. 7
Charlotte, VT 05445
(802) 425-3500
Excellent wildflower seed and seed mixes.

Wayside Gardens
Garden Lande
Hodges, SC 29695
Offers a wide array of bulbs and perennials.

We-Du Nurseries
Rt. 5 Box 724
Marion, NC 28752
(704) 738-8300
Incredible variety of wildflowers and native perennials from several continents, many woodland plants.

Westgate Garden Nursery
751 Westgate Drive
Eureka, CA 95503
Large selection of rhododendrons and unusual ornamental shrubs and trees.

White Flower Farm
P.O. Box 50
Litchfield, CT 06759
(800) 503-9624
Good selection of plants, including hostas, ferns, and hellebores.

Wildlife Nurseries
P.O. Box 2724
Oshkosh, WI 54903
(414) 231-3780
Plants and seeds of native grasses, annuals, and perennials for wildlife. Also water garden plants and supplies.

Wildwood Gardens
14488 Rock Creek Road
Chardon, OH 44024
Collector's list of dwarf conifers and other dwarf shrubs.

Woodlanders, Inc.
1128 Colleton Ave.
Aiken, SC 29801
(803) 648-7522
Excellent selection of native trees, shrubs, ferns, vines, and perennials, plus other good garden plants.

Yucca Do Nursery
P.O. Box 655
Waller, TX 77484
(409) 826-6363
Good selection of trees, shrubs, and perennial plants, including many natives.

GARDEN ACCENTS

Anderson Design
P.O. Box 4057 C
Bellingham, WA 98227
(800) 947-7697
Arbors, trellises, gates, and pyramids (Oriental, modern, and traditional style).

Bamboo Fencer
31 Germania Street
Jamaica Plain, Boston, MA 02130
(617) 524-6137
Bamboo fences.

Barlow Tyrie Inc.
1263 Glen Avenue Suite 230
Moorestown, NJ 08057-1139
(609) 273-7878
Teak wood garden furniture in English garden style.

Boston Turning Works
42 Plymouth Street
Boston, MA 02118
(617) 482-9085
Distinctive wood finials for gates, fenceposts, and balustrades.

Brooks Barrel Company
P.O. Box 1056
Department GD25
Cambridge, MD 21613-1046
(410) 228-0790
Natural-finish pine wooden barrels and planters.

Charleston Gardens
61 Queen Street
Charleston, SC 29401
(803) 723-0252
Fine garden furnishings.

Doner Design Inc.
Department G
2175 Beaver Valley Pike
New Providence, PA 17560
(717) 786-8891
Handcrafted copper landscape lights.

Florentine Craftsmen Inc.
46–24 28th Street
Department GD
Long Island City, NY 11101
(718) 937-7632
Garden furniture, ornaments, fountains and statuary of lead, stone, and bronze.

Flower Framers by Jay
671 Wilmer Avenue
Cincinnati, Ohio 45226
Flower boxes.

FrenchWyres
P.O. Box 131655
Tyler, TX 75713
(903) 597-8322
Wire garden furnishings: trellis, urns, cachepots, window boxes, arches, and plant stands.

Gardenia
9 Remington Street
Cambridge, MA 02138
(800) 685-8866
Birdhouses.

Gardensheds
651 Millcross Road
Lancaster, PA 17601
Potting sheds, wood boxes, and larger storage units.

Hooks Lattice
7949 Silverton Avenue #903
San Diego, CA 92126
(800) 896-0978
Handcrafted wrought-iron gardenware.

Kenneth Lynch & Sons
84 Danbury ROad
P.O. Box 488
Wilton, CT 06897
(203) 762-8363
Benches, gates, sculpture and statuary, planters and urns, topiary, sundials, and weathervanes.

Kinsman Company
River Road
Department 351
Point Pleasant, PA 18950
(800) 733-4146
European plant supports, pillars, arches trellises, flowerpots, and planters.

Lake Creek Garden Features Inc.
P.O. Box 118
Lake City, IA 51449
(712) 464-8924
Obelisks, plant stands, and gazing globes and stands.

Liteform Designs
P.O. Box 3316
Portland, OR 97208
(503) 253-1210
Garden lighting: path, bullard, accent, step, and tree fixtures.

New Blue Moon Studio
P.O. Box 579
Leavenworth, WA 98826
(509) 548-4754
Trellises, gates, arbors, and garden furniture.

New England Garden
Ornaments
P.O. Box 235
38 East Brookfield Road
North Brookfield, MA 01535
(508) 867-4474
Garden fountains and statuary, planters and urns, antique furniture, sundials, and limestone ornaments.

Secret Garden
c/o Christine Sibley
15 Waddell Street N.E.
Atlanta, GA 30307
Garden sculpture.

Stone Forest
Department G
P.O. Box 2840
Sante Fe, NM 87504
(505) 986-8883
Hand-carved granite birdbaths, basins, fountains, lanterns, and spheres.

Sycamore Creek
P.O. Box 16
Ancram, NY 12502
Handcrafted copper garden furnishings.

Tanglewood Conservatories
Silver Spring, MD
Handcrafted period glass houses and atriums.

Tidewater Workshop
Oceanville, NJ 08231
(800) 666-8433
White cedar benches, chairs, swings, and tables.

Toscano
17 East Campbell Street
Department G881
Arlington Heights, IL 60005
(800) 525-1733
Historic garden sculptures, including seraphs and cherubs.

Valcovic Cornell Design
Box 380
Beverly, MA 01915
Trellises and arbor benches (traditional to contemporary styles).

Vixen Hill Manufacturing
    Company
Main Street
Elverson, PA 19520
(800) 423-2766
Cedar gazebos and screened garden houses.

Weatherend Estate Furniture
6 Gordon Drive
Rockland, ME 04841
(800) 456-6483
Heirloom-quality garden furniture.

Wood Classics
Box 96G0410
Gardiner, NY 12525
(914) 255-5651
Garden benches, swings, chairs and tables, rockers, lounges, and umbrellas (all teak and mahogany outdoor furniture).

AUSTRALIA

Country Farm Perennials
RSD Laings Road
Nayook VIC 3821

Cox's Nursery
RMB 216 Oaks Road
Thrilmere NSW 2572

Honeysuckle Cottage Nursery
Lot 35 Bowen Mountain Road
Bowen Mountain via Grosevale
NSW 2753

Swan Bros Pty Ltd
490 Galston Road
Dural NSW 2158

CANADA

Corn Hill Nursery Ltd.
RR 5
Petitcodiac NB EOA 2HO

Ferncliff Gardens
SS 1
Mission, British Columbia
V2V 5V6

McFayden Seed Co. Ltd.
Box 1800
Brandon, Manitoba
R7A 6N4

Stirling Perennials
RR 1
Morpeth, Ontario
NOP 1X0

PHOTO CREDITS

©Rob Cardillo: pp. 56 top, 61 left, 94 top, 107 top, 133 top, 133 bottom

©David Cavagnaro: pp. 25, 44 bottom, 54, 57, 58, 59 bottom, 61 right, 81 top, 82 top, 82 bottom, 95 top, 106

©Todd Davis: pp. 34 bottom, 70, 81 bottom, 85 bottom, 116

©Brian Durell: pp. 56 bottom, 85 top, 93, 117 bottom

©Derek Fell: pp. 24, 37 bottom, 73

The Garden Picture Library:
©John Glover: pp. 27, 122;
©Sunniva Harte: 131 top;
©LaMontagne: p. 107 bottom;
©Marie O'Hara: pp. 46 top;
©Howard Rice: pp. 35 top;
©JS Sira: p. 47 top

©John Glover: pp. 2, 26, 37 top, 92, 97, 109

©Dency Kane: pp.10, 45, 55, 80, 84 bottom

©Donna and Tom Krischan: pp. 15, 35 bottom, 47 bottom, 62, 72 right, 84 top, 96 top, 120, 130

©Charles Mann: pp. 108

©Ken Meyer: pp. 132 left

©Jerry Pavia: pp. 12,16, 36, 60, 72 left, 95 bottom, 105, 118, 119 right, 121 bottom, 132 right

©Cheryl Richter: pp. 34 top, 44 top, 46 bottom, 71, 96 bottom, 104 top, 104 bottom, 123, 131 bottom

©Aleksandra Szywala: pp. 83, 117 top, 119 left, 121 top

©Mark Turner: pp. 94 bottom

©Rick Wetherbee: pp. 59 top, 63

©Judy White/GardenPhotos.com: p. 8

INDEX

Accents, garden, 36

African daisy (*Arctotis stoechadifolia*), 133

Alberta spruce, 22

Allium schoenoprasum (chives), 62, 84

Alyssum (*Lobularia maritima*), 25
purple, 96
white, 94

Annuals, 15

Anthemum graveolens (dill), 81

Arctotis stoechadifolia (African daisy), 133

Athyrium nipponicum 'Pictum' (Japanese painted fern), 117

Basil (*Ocimum basilicum*), 84

Bell pepper, 61

Biennials, 15

Bleeding heart, wild (*Dicentra eximia*), 117

Boston fern (*Nephrolepis exaltata* 'Bostoniensis'), 119

Boxwood (*Buxus* spp.), topiary, 26

Buddleia davidii (butterfly bush), 44
cutting back, 42

Bulbs, 15

Bush basil (*Ocimum minimum*), 84

Busy lizzies (*Impatiens wallerana*), 121

Butterfly bush (*Buddleia davidii*), 44
cutting back, 42

Butterfly garden, 39–47

Caladium (*Caladium* spp.), 118

Catmint (*Nepeta* x *faassenii*), 47

Cattail, dwarf (*Typha* 'Minima'), 73

Celosia (*Celosia* spp.), 104

Chamomile (*Chamaemelum nobile*), 81

Cherry tomatoes, 55

Children's vegetable garden, 49–63

Chives (*Allium schoenoprasum*), 62, 84

Chrysanthemum frutescens (marguerite daisies), 24

Cilantro (*Coriandrum sativum*), 78

Coleus (*Coleus* spp.), 120

Colorful garden, 99–109

Containers
choosing, 10–11
cleaning, 11
for windowsills, 128

Coral bells (*Heuchera* spp.), 119

Coriandrum sativum (Cilantro), 78

Cottage pink (*Dianthus plumarius*), 94

Cymbopogon citratus (lemongrass), 78

Dahlia (*Dahlia* spp.), 109
'All Triumph', 34

Daisy
African (*Arctotis stoechadifolia*), 133
marguerite (*Chrysanthemum frutescens*), 24

Deadheading, 15, 17

Dianthus plumarius (cottage pink), 94

Dibble, 17

Dicentra eximia (wild bleeding heart), 117

Dill (*Anthemum graveolens*), 81

Dwarf cattail (*Typha* 'Minima'), 73

Dwarf sunflower (*Helianthus*), 58

Eggplant, 59

Eichhornia crassipes (water hyacinth), 72

Entry garden, formal, 19–27

Evergreen shrubs, 19

Evergreen topiaries, 19, 22

Fennel (*Foeniculum vulgare*), 78

Fern
Boston (*Nephrolepis exaltata* 'Bostoniensis'), 119
Japanese painted (*Athyrium nipponicum* 'Pictum'), 117

Fertilizing, 13–14

Fish, in water garden, 68

Floral snips, 17

Foeniculum vulgare (fennel), 78

Formal entry garden, 19–27

Fragrant garden, 87–97

French marigold (*Tagetes patula*), 104

Fuchsia (*Fuchsia* spp.), 24, 45, 121

Geranium (*Pelargonium* spp.), 130
classic (*Pelargonium* x *hortorum*), 106
ivy (*Pelargonium peltatum*), 107
scented, 96

Greek oregano (*Origanum vulgare* spp. *hirtum*), 85

Hedera (ivy), variegated, 27, 37, 122

Helianthus (sunflower), dwarf, 58

Helichrysum (*Helichrysum petiolatum*), 132
  variegated (*Helichrysum petiolare* 'Variegatum'), 36
Heliotrope (*Heliotropium* spp.), 29, 35, 95, 132
Herbs, 75–85
  basil (*Ocimum basilicum*), 84
  catmint (*Nepeta x faassenii*), 47
  chamomile (*Chamaemelum nobile*), 81
  chives (*Allium schoenoprasum*), 62, 84
  cilantro (*Coriandrum sativum*), 78
  dill (*Anthemum graveolens*), 81
  fennel (*Foeniculum vulgare*), 78
  lavender (*Lavandula angustifolia*), 93
  lemon basil (*Ocimum basilicum citriodorum*), 84
  lemongrass (*Cymbopogon citratus*), 78
  marjoram (*Origanum majorana*), 78
  mint (*Mentha* spp.), 78
  oregano, Greek/golden (*Origanum vulgare* spp. hirtum), 85
  parsley (*Petrolinum crispum*), 63, 82
  pinching back, 79
  rosemary (*Rosmarinus officinalis*), 75, 80
  sage (*Salvia officinalis*), 85

summer savory (*Satureja hortensis*), 78
thyme (*Thymus vulgaris*), 82
Heuchera spp. (coral bells), 119
Hibiscus (*Hibiscus* spp.), 24
Hibiscus moscheutos (rose mallow), 47
Holly, San Jose, 22
Hosta (*Hosta* spp.), 116
Hummingbird garden, 39–47
Hyacinth, water, (*Eichhornia crassipes*), 72

Impatiens wallerana (busy lizzies), 121
Impatiens x hawkeri (New Guinea impatiens), 121
Ipomea alba (moonflower), 34
Ipomoea batatas (sweet potato vine), 122
Ivy (*Hedera* spp.), variegated, 27, 37, 122
Ivy geranium (*Pelargonium peltatum*), 107

Japanese painted fern (*Athyrium nipponicum* 'Pictum'), 117
Juniper, 22

Lavender (*Lavandula angustifolia*), 93
Lemon basil (*Ocimum basilicum citriodorum*), 84
Lemongrass (*Cymbopogon citratus*), 78
Lettuce mix, 57
Licorice plant, 36, 132

Lily (*Lilium*), Star Gazer, 97. See also Water lily
Lobelia (*Lobelia erinus*), 131
Lobularia maritima (alyssum), 25
  purple, 96
  white, 94

Marguerite daisies (*Chrysanthemum frutescens*), 24
Marigold, French (*Tagetes patula*), 104
Marjoram (*Origanum majorana*), 78
Markers, making, 53
Mint (*Mentha* spp.), 78
Moon garden, 29–37
Moonflower (*Ipomea alba*), 34
Myriophyllum aquaticum (parrot's feather), 72

Nasturtium (*Tropaeolum majus*), 60, 83, 105
  seed planting of, 99
Nepeta x faassenii (catmint), 47
Nephrolepis exaltata 'Bostoniensis' (Boston fern), 119
New Guinea impatiens (*Impatiens x hawkeri*), 121
Nicotiana alata (flowering tobacco), 95
  'Apple Blossom,' 35
Nymphaea (water lily), 70
  overwintering of, 69
  substitute for, 71

Ocimum basilicum (basil), 84
Oregano, Greek/golden (*Origanum vulgare* spp. hirtum), 85
Origanum majorana (marjoram), 78
Origanum vulgare spp. hirtum (Greek/golden oregano), 85
Ornaments, garden, 36

Parrot's feather (*Myriophyllum aquaticum*), 72
Parsley (*Petrolinum crispum*), 63, 82
Peas, 56
Pelargonium (geranium), 130
  classic (*Pelargonium x hortorum*), 106
  ivy (*Pelargonium peltatum*), 107
  scented, 96
Pepper, bell, 61
Perennials, 15
Petrolinum crispum (parsley), 63, 82
Petunia (*Petunia x hybrida*), 37, 44
Plant hardiness zones, 15–16, 134
Planting, 11–12
Pole beans, 54
Potting mixes, choosing, 10
Pruning, 14
  rose, 90